The Hou

MW00944649

Compiled by Ruth Lambert
with Henry S. Harrison

Edited by Angela Hulford
Design & Layout by Blaine Kruger

Text and illustrations used
with permission from
Houses: *The Illustrated Guide to*
Construction, Design and Systems
by Henry S. Harrison

COPYRIGHT

PREFACE & ACKNOWLEDGMENTS

This book was developed and planned many years ago in the kitchen of our Victorian brownstone on Court Street in downtown New Haven, Connecticut. I sat reading aloud from a cookbook while Henry, my fiancé, was making dinner. When I turned to the index, I noticed an entry for Adobe Bread. As I read the name aloud, we experienced one of those magical moments of telepathy: our conversation consisted entirely of two-word phrases. "Let's put together --" "A cookbook!" "Based on all the House styles --" "In your Houses book." We laughed, and this idea was born.

Now we're married over forty years, with four children (two from my husband's first marriage), six grandchildren, and good friends and loving family who've tasted and enjoyed the recipes in this cookbook. Thanks to all the kind people everywhere who shared their favorite recipes with us.

I especially appreciated the organizational help of friends Sue Testa and Myra Zelson, who worked with me at the very beginning of this project. My assistant Angie Hulford spent about a year typing, editing and compiling the manuscript, and graphic designer Blaine Kruger helped make the book easy to use and fun to look at. Jean Liskow did her usual superior job of proofreading. Warm fuzzies to all. Special thanks to my husband, friend and collaborator, Henry S. Harrison, who trusted me to turn our shared idea into this reality.

We used the beautiful illustrations by California-based artist Josef Jaqua from Henry's book **Houses** throughout this book. We've had a lot of fun over the past four decades with this cookbook, which has become a traditional family gift for friends, teachers and thousands of customers around the country. They tell us the Adobe Chicken recipe is the best.

We hope you will enjoy it, too. Bon appetite!

Ruth Lambert
January 2018

iii

DEDICATION

In loving memory of my
dear parents-in-law,
"Julie" & Helen Harrison,
who always hoped I'd start cooking,
and in honor of my beloved parents,
the late Joseph M. Lambert, aka "Dodi"
and Rochelle R. Lambert,
who never thought there was
anything I couldn't do.

AUTHOR'S NOTE

The organization of this book follows the major architectural periods and styles of houses featured in my husband's best-selling book **Houses**: *The Illustrated Guide to Construction, Design and Systems.*

A sample menu precedes each section to provide a unifying theme for the recipes which follow. The Index of Recipes is arranged by food group (e.g., "Egg Dishes") and the part of the meal involved (e.g., "Appetizers"), for easy reference.

We've included quite a few vegetarian dishes, in keeping with the lighter, healthier fare Americans are eating these days. I hope you will enjoy our Cookbook and want to share it with others.

Ruth Lambert
January 2018

LIST OF HOUSE STYLES

Colonial American

English

French

Swiss

Latin

Oriental

19th Century American

Early 20th Century American

Post World War II American

TABLE OF CONTENTS

NEW ENGLAND DINNER

New England is known for great seafood from the abundant Atlantic Ocean usually served with creative side-dishes featuring farm-fresh produce from neighboring areas.

Many food traditions have started in New England. At the turn of the century, Election Day was a special event. After a trip to the polls, people met in groups to celebrate victory or commiserate over defeat. Guests were served a traditional rich yeast-based cake, which originated in Hartford, Connecticut. Punch and eggnog were always served along with Election Day Cake.

FEDERAL STYLE

Prevalent throughout America's eastern cities in the 1700's, this elegant style takes on many forms. Some authorities consider the Federal and Adams styles to be the same.

The Federal is a multi-story, symmetrical box-shaped house with a flat roof, small-paned glass windows, and one or more protruding chimneys. Clapboard or brick are used to construct the exterior walls. Typically, a belvedere and a balustrade help define this beautifully ornamented house style.

Election Day Coffee Cake
Serves 10-12

INGREDIENTS

1/2	c.	warm water
2	pkgs.	active dry yeast
1/2	c.	milk, scalded and cooled
3 1/4	c.	sifted all-purpose flour
1/2	t.	salt
2	t.	cinnamon
1/4	t.	mace
1/2	t.	nutmeg
1/4	t.	ground cloves
1/2	c.	butter
3/4	c.	sugar
3		eggs, well beaten
1	c.	chopped nuts
1/2	c.	candied citron chopped

DIRECTIONS

Soften yeast in a bowl of warm water.

Stir the lukewarm milk into the yeast.

Add gradually 1-1/2 cups of the flour, beating well after each addition. Beat until smooth.

Cover the bowl with wax paper and a clean towel. Let it rise in a warm place (80 degrees F.) for about 45 minutes.

Sift together the remaining flour, salt, and spices. Set aside.

Cream the butter until softened.

Add the sugar gradually, creaming until fluffy.

Add the beaten eggs gradually, beating well after each addition.

Blend in the yeast mixture.

Add the dry ingredients, beating until smooth.

Mix in the chopped nuts and citron.

Grease the bottom of a 9-inch tube pan.

Turn mixture into the pan and cover with wax paper and a towel and let it rise again, away from drafts, until the pan is almost full -- about 2 hours.

Bake at 350 degrees for 50 minutes.

Remove from the oven to a wire rack and cool 10 minutes in the pan.

Invert cake onto a wire rack and cool completely before slicing.

Preparation time: 3-1/2 hrs.
Total time: 6-1/2 hours
Skill level: Intermediate

3

NEW ENGLAND FARMHOUSE

These attractive houses were built in the 1700's and 1800's throughout New England. They were a great favorite among farmers who could not afford the more elaborate styles of the times. They were designed using common building materials and techniques of the period, were simple to construct and easy to maintain.

The New England Farmhouse is a simple, box-shaped house. Traditional exterior siding material is white clapboard. A steep pitched roof sheds heavy snow and a central chimney supports the frame.

Green Beans with Tomatoes
Serves 8

INGREDIENTS

1 1/2	lbs. fresh green beans, cut
3	T. butter or margarine
1/2	c. chopped onions
2	T. flour
1/4	t. salt
1/8	t. pepper
1 1/4	c. milk
2 1/2	c. grated sharp cheese
2	ripe tomatoes, sliced

DIRECTIONS

Cook the beans in boiling water until they are tender; drain and keep hot.
Melt the butter in a saucepan over medium heat.
Add the onions and sauté until golden.
Stir in the flour, salt and pepper to make a smooth paste.
Add the milk gradually and cook, stirring until thickened.
Add the cheese and stir until melted.
Grease the bottom of a 2-quart casserole dish; place hot green beans in the dish.
Pour 3/4 of the cheese sauce over the green beans.
Cover the beans with the tomato slices.
Sprinkle lightly with salt and top with the rest of the cheese sauce.
Place under the broiler for 5 minutes until the tomatoes are tender and the cheese sauce is bubbling and golden brown.

Preparation time: 45 min.
Total time: 45 minutes
Skill level: Elementary

5

ADAMS COLONIAL

Introduced by Robert Adam in 1759 upon his return from a trip to Europe, this handsome style was launched in New England where it was promoted by two famous early architects, Charles Bulfinch and Samuel McIntire.

A rectangular multi-story house of classic beauty, the Adams Colonial has large bay windows. Its chimneys protrude through a flat roof which is topped with a balustrade. The over-all effect is one of lightness and delicacy. The entrance steps are finished with light iron rails and there are fantail windows on either side and above the front door.

Apple Fritters
Serves 8

INGREDIENTS

Fat or oil for frying.
1   c. all-purpose flour
1   t. baking powder
1/2 t. salt
1   egg, well beaten
1   c. milk
4   T. sugar
1/4 t. cinnamon
2   c. apples, pared,
        and chopped
Confectioner's sugar

DIRECTIONS

Heat fat or oil (3 to 4 inches) to 375 degrees in deep fryer or kettle.
Sift together the flour, baking powder and salt .
Add the egg and the milk.
Mix until smooth.
Add the sugar, cinnamon and apples.
Stir to blend well.
Drop batter by level tablespoons into the hot fat and fry about 5 minutes or until thoroughly cooked.
Drain on paper towels.
Sprinkle with confectioner's sugar.

Preparation time: 45 min.
Total time: 45 minutes
Skill level: Elementary

CAPE COD COLONIAL

The Cape Cod Colonial is the earliest architectural style that is still popular today. It was the most popular house style in America from the mid-1920's through the late 1950's and is found throughout the country.

A small, symmetrical, 1-1/2-story compact house with a central entrance, the Cape Cod features a steep gable roof covered with shingles. Authentic Cape Cod Colonials have low central chimneys, but end chimneys are very common in the newer versions. Originally, the exterior walls were white clapboard, natural shingles or brick, but modern versions often use other siding materials. A simple cornice with gutters overhangs the first floor double-hung windows.

Baked Stuffed Cod Fish
Serves 8-10

INGREDIENTS

1		6-to 8-pound Cod fish, cleaned
		salt and pepper
		Mushroom Stuffing
		salad oil
1/2	c.	melted butter or margarine
3	T.	lemon juice

Mushroom Stuffing

1/2	c.	chopped onions
1/4	c.	butter or margarine
1 1/2	c.	dry bread cubes
1	c.	cut-up fresh mushrooms
1/4	c.	snipped parsley
1		clove garlic, minced
1	T.	lemon juice
1		egg
1	t.	salt
1/4	t.	thyme
1/4	t.	pepper

DIRECTIONS

Preheat the oven to 350 degrees.
Prepare the mushroom stuffing (see below) and set aside.
Wash the fish in cold water; pat dry.
Rub the cavity with salt and pepper.
Stuff the cavity with the stuffing.
Close the opening with skewers and lace with string. (Extra stuffing may be placed in a covered baking dish and placed in the oven 20 minutes before serving).
Brush the fish with salad oil and place in a shallow, open roasting pan.
Mix butter and lemon juice together and baste the fish occasionally.
Bake about 1 hour or until the fish flakes easily with a fork.

Mushroom Stuffing

Cook and stir the onion in butter until tender.
Mix in remaining ingredients.

Preparation time: 20 min.
Total time: 1 hour, 20 min.
Skill level: Elementary

9

CAPE ANN COLONIAL

This house is a variety of the Cape Cod style popular in the Cape Ann area of Massachusetts. A small, symmetrical, 1-1/2-story, compact house with a central entrance, the Cape Ann is distinguished by its shingle-covered gambrel roof.

Traditionally, the exterior walls are white clapboard or natural shingles. Other characteristics of the Cape Ann include double-hung windows, shutters the same length as the windows, and a simple cornice with gutters immediately above the first floor windows. The floor plan requires walking through one room to reach another and features several bedrooms on the first floor. The attic may include additional bedrooms and a bath.

Bay Scallop Bisque
Serves 6-8

INGREDIENTS

1 1/2	lbs. bay scallops
1/2	stick butter
1/2	t. tarragon or dill weed
2	c. white wine or clam juice
2	c. light cream

DIRECTIONS

Cook the scallops gently in butter in a skillet over medium heat until opaque in color (about 4 minutes). **Stir** in the tarragon or dill weed and cook for 1 minute. **Stir** in the wine and cream. **Turn** up the heat, and warm until mixture just comes to a simmer.

Preparation time: 20 min.
Total time: 20 minutes
Skill level: Elementary

Notes

HARVEST DINNER

Tomatoes with Feta Cheese	p. 25
Cheese & Vegetable Chowder	p. 17
Corned Beef Brisket	p. 21
Maple Acorn Squash	p. 15
Hot German Potato Salad	p. 23
Dutch Apple Pie	p. 19

In earlier times, it was the custom to have a harvest social to celebrate the completion of all the hard work of the planting and reaping seasons. There was usually little socializing possible due to demanding farm-related responsibilities. The Harvest Dinner was a welcome opportunity for neighbors to come together for conversation and good food. Foods from homemade Apple pie to Zucchini casserole were served to all.

This celebration was not only a time to share the bounty of the land; it was also an outward expression of thankfulness for good friends, freedom from want, and peace.

GARRISON COLONIAL

The Garrison Colonial is named after block-houses used during the Colonial era to fend off Indians, but the overhang style is probably related to the Elizabethan townhouse. The ends of the framing beams form the carved drops on early versions of the house. Later, they were added for decoration. Examples of this style built in the 1600's are still standing today.

This symmetrical 2-1/2 story house features the second-story overhang in front. Traditional ornamentation includes four carved pineapple or acorn-shaped drops below the overhang. The second story windows are often smaller than those on the first floor and dormers may break through the cornice line.

Maple Acorn Squash
Serves 8

INGREDIENTS

4	acorn squash
	rosemary
	salt
1/3	c. maple syrup

DIRECTIONS

Preheat the oven to 400 degrees.

Split the squash; remove and discard the seeds.

Sprinkle the cut side of each squash lightly with rosemary and salt.

Turn the squash cut side down in a baking pan.

Surround the acorn squash with 1/2 inch of hot water.

Bake uncovered in a 400 degree oven for about 45 minutes or until tender.

Turn the squash cut side up.

Spoon 2 teaspoons of maple syrup into each cavity and spread to coat all surfaces.

Return the squash to the oven for 5 minutes.

Preparation time: 15 min.
Total time: 65 minutes
Skill level: Elementary

NEW ENGLAND COLONIAL

These large and roomy houses evolved from the Cape Cod style. The New England Colonial is a 2-1/2-story, generally symmetrical, square or rectangular house with side or rear wings. The traditional material is narrow clapboard siding. The gable roof is usually shingled.

Originally the style had chimneys at each end for heating purposes, but modern versions have only one chimney. The house features an elaborate cornice with dentils. Windows are double-hung with small glass panes and shutters the same size as the windows. The central entrance often has side lights and a fan light. A central hallway on the first floor runs from the front of the house to the rear making for easy, free-flowing access.

Cheese and Vegetable Chowder
Serves 6-8

INGREDIENTS

4	T. butter or margarine
1/4	c. finely chopped onion
1	c. chopped green pepper
1	c. pared sliced carrot
1	pkg. (10 oz.) frozen peas
5	T. flour
	chopped parsley
2	cans (10-3/4 oz.) condensed chicken broth, undiluted
3	c. grated sharp cheddar cheese
2	c. milk
1/4	t. salt
	dash pepper
1/2	c. croutons (optional)

DIRECTIONS

Melt the butter in a 3 quart saucepan.

Place the vegetables in the saucepan; cook covered for 20 to 25 minutes 'til tender, stirring occasionally.

Remove from heat.

Stir in the flour and mix well.

Cook 1 minute, stirring occasionally.

Add the chicken broth to vegetable mixture.

Bring to a boil, stirring constantly. Lower heat.

Stir in cheese gradually.

Cook over medium heat, stirring until the cheese has melted.

Add the milk gradually.

Season with salt and pepper.

Bring just to steaming (do not boil).

Sprinkle with parsley and serve with croutons.

Note: This chowder can be made the day before and reheated.

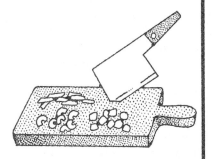

Preparation time: 1-1/2 hrs.
Total time: 1-1/2 hours
Skill level: Elementary

DUTCH COLONIAL

This native American style did not originate in Holland. German settlers built them in Pennsylvania in the 1600's and soon after in New York. The name "Deutsch", which means German, was mispronounced and misspelled as Dutch.

The Dutch Colonial is a 2 to 2-1/2 story house with a gambrel roof and eaves that flare outward. Second story dormers through the roof are common and the chimney is usually off-center. The exterior may be made of a wide variety of material such as clapboard, shingles, cut stone, brick or stucco. Other features include double-hung windows with small panes of glass and a split entrance door.

Dutch Apple Pie
Serves 8

INGREDIENTS

Pastry for 9-inch two-crust pie (frozen)
3/4 c. sugar
1/2 c. all-purpose flour
1/2 t. nutmeg
3/4 t. cinnamon
6 c. thinly sliced and pared apples
2 T. butter or margarine
1/2 c. whipping cream

DIRECTIONS

Preheat the oven to 425 degrees.

Thaw the pastry shell and top crust.

Stir together sugar, flour, nutmeg, and cinnamon.

Mix gently with the apples.

Turn into the 9-inch pie shell.

Dot with butter.

Cover with the top crust.

Cut large slits in the top of the crust with a knife.

Seal the top and bottom crusts together and flute the edge by pinching.

Cover the edges with a 2-inch strip of aluminum foil to prevent excessive browning; remove foil during the last 15 minutes of baking.

Pour the whipping cream through the slits in the top crust 5 minutes before pie is finished baking.

Bake 40 to 50 minutes or until the crust is brown.

Preparation time: 40 min.
Total time: 90 minutes
Skill level: Elementary

19

SALT BOX OR CATSLIDE

The Salt Box or Catslide is a Colonial New England farmhouse with a lean-to shed or room added to the rear of the house. This room is oriented to the north and has no windows, to create a buffer against cold winter winds. The house resembles the old-fashioned salt boxes found in country stores.

A 2 or 2-1/2 story house, a Salt Box is square or rectangular in shape, with a steep gable roof that extends down to the first floor in the rear. In order to obtain the traditional lean-to look, headroom in the rear must be sacrificed. Exterior walls are usually clapboard or shingles and a large chimney protrudes from the center of the house. Windows are large and double-hung with small panes of glass and shutters the same size as the windows.

Corned Beef Brisket
Serves 8-10

INGREDIENTS

5 lb corned beef brisket
     (well-trimmed)
2 onions, quartered
1 garlic clove, crushed
3 sprigs thyme, chopped
3 sprigs parsley, chopped
3 bay leaves

DIRECTIONS

Place the meat in a large kettle.
Cover with cold water.
Add the remaining ingredients.
Heat to boiling.
Reduce the heat and cover tightly.
Simmer for about 3-1/2 hours
or until tender. If necessary, skim
off any foam which may float to the
top during cooking.
Take the meat out when it is done
and let it stand for 10 minutes.
Carve meat by cutting thin diagonal
slices across the grain.
Serve on a platter.

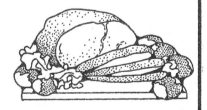

Preparation time: 5 min.
Total time: 3 hours, 35 min.
Skill level: Elementary

21

PENNSYLVANIA DUTCH COLONIAL

This style, also known as a Pennsylvania German Farmhouse, was first built in the mid-1600's west of Philadelphia on the Main Line and in Lancaster, Pennsylvania. The name also derives from the mispronunciation of the word "Deutsch" since they were first built by people of German origin.

A massive 2-1/2-story gray ledge-stone house with a steep gable roof, it features a traditional unsupported hood over the front entrance. When wings are added they are usually partly clapboard. Other characteristics include a shingle roof, and double-hung windows with small panes of glass. Thousands of these handsome homes are still in use in the area around Philadelphia.

Hot German Potato Salad
Serves 8

INGREDIENTS

8	medium potatoes
6	slices bacon
3/4	c. chopped onion
3/4	c. chopped celery
1 1/2	c. water
2/3	c. cider vinegar
1/2	c. sugar
2	t. salt
1/4	t. pepper
1/2	c. sliced radishes

DIRECTIONS

Wash and pare potatoes.
Boil in water until tender but not soft.
Drain and slice.
Pan-fry the bacon in a skillet; drain and crumble.
Pour off excess drippings; reserve 1/4 cup in the skillet.
Sauté the onion and celery in the bacon fat until tender.
Blend in the flour.
Stir in the water and vinegar.
Cook, stirring constantly until the mixture is thick and bubbly.
Stir in the sugar, salt and pepper. Mix well.
Place potatoes in a 3-quart casserole; sprinkle with the bacon.
Pour the hot mixture over the potatoes and cover.
Bake at 350 degrees for 30 minutes.
Remove from the oven and stir in the sliced radishes.

Preparation time: 1 hour
Total time: 1-1/2 hours
Skill level: Elementary

CLASSIC
COLONIAL

Based on classic Greek architecture, this style was introduced by Thomas Jefferson who built Monticello in 1772 and remodeled it several times until 1803. There is very little difference between a Classic Colonial and a Greek Revival and many architectural historians use the terms synonomously.

A large, impressive showplace, the Classic Colonial is a 2 or 3-story house with a columned exterior. The columns have Doric, Ionic or Corinthian capitals. Pilasters in the walls are common and there are various roof shapes on the same house. A portico at one entrance, with a roof supported by columns, is a traditional feature of this style.

Tomatoes with Feta Cheese
Serves 8

INGREDIENTS

4 large ripe tomatoes
1 c. crumbled feta cheese
1 t. oregano
   salt and pepper

DIRECTIONS

Slice the tomatoes in half.
Sprinkle each tomato half with about 2 tablespoons of cheese and some of the oregano, salt and pepper.
Broil for 5 to 10 minutes and serve immediately.

Preparation time: 10 min.
Total time: 20 minutes
Skill level: Elementary

Notes

SPRING RECEPTION

Greek Salad	p. 29
Caraway Cheese Log	p. 35
Cold Boiled Lobster Salad	p. 33
Pecan Tarts	p. 31
Orange Sherbet	p. 36
Lemonade Ice Tea	p. 37

A springtime reception is a lovely way to welcome beautiful weather and celebrate a special occasion at the same time.

This charming, light meal can be served on a Sunday afternoon in place of the more traditional Sunday Dinner. It is also delightful after a recital, Christening or small informal wedding.

GREEK REVIVAL

There is little difference between a Greek Revival and a Classic Colonial. Architectural historians often consider them to be the same style. For clarity of identification, the houses that look like traditional Greek temples are generally called Greek Revival. The style became popular in the U.S. in the early 1800's, especially for public buildings.

The Greek Revival style is a 2-story or 3-story, symmetrical house that copies the style of a Greek temple, complete with columns, architraves, friezes and cornices. The windows are small and hidden as they are not part of classic Greek temple architecture.

Greek Salad
Serves 12

INGREDIENTS

2	heads iceberg lettuce
2	heads chicory
4	tomatoes, cut in wedges
3	green onions, finely chopped
1	c. Greek olives
1/2	c. olive oil
1/2	c. salad oil
1/3	c. wine vinegar
1	t. salt
	Freshly ground pepper to taste
1/2	t. dry mustard
2	t. oregano
1/2	lb. feta cheese, crumbled
4	oz. anchovy fillets

DIRECTIONS

Tear lettuce and chicory into pieces and place in a large salad bowl.

Add the tomatoes, onions, olives, and feta cheese, reserving 4 tablespoons of cheese for a garnish. Toss gently.

Shake together the olive and salad oils, vinegar, salt, pepper, dry mustard, and oregano until well blended.

Pour the dressing over the salad just before serving and toss.

Sprinkle with the reserved feta cheese and top with the anchovy fillets.

Preparation time: 30 min.
Total time: 30 minutes
Skill level: Elementary

SOUTHERN COLONIAL

This style is a Southern interpretation of the New England Colonial, modified to suit the warmer climate. The classic example pictured here is Mount Vernon, home of George Washington, built in the 1700's.

This is a large 2 or 3-story frame house with a colonnade extending across the front. The hip or gable shingle roof extends over the colonnade. Other distinguishing characteristics include a second-story balcony, cornices with dentils, a belvedere and balustrade and double-hung windows with small panes of glass. These homes are spacious, symmetrical and very appealing to the eye.

Pecan Tarts
Yield: 12 tarts

INGREDIENTS

2	pkgs. pie crust mix
3	eggs, slightly beaten
1	c. corn syrup
1	c. sugar
2	T. melted butter or margarine
1/2	t. vanilla
1 1/2	c. pecan halves
	whipped cream

DIRECTIONS

Preheat the oven to 350 degrees.

Prepare the pastry for a two-crust pie as directed on the package.

Divide the pastry into 12 equal portions.

Shape each portion into a ball.

Roll each piece into a 4-inch circle on a lightly floured surface.

Place each pastry circle into a muffin cup, making pleats so the pastry will fit. (Do not prick.)

Stir together the eggs, corn syrup, sugar, butter and vanilla until blended.

Add the nuts.

Pour the filling into the pastry-lined muffin cups.

Bake about 40 minutes, until the filling is set and the pastry is lightly browned.

Cool and serve with whipped cream.

Note: The pecan filling recipe may be doubled or tripled. However, prepare only enough pastry for about 12 tarts at a time, as it will be easier to work.

Preparation time: 1 hour
Total time: 1 hour, 40 min.
Skill level: Intermediate

31

FRONT GABLE OR CHARLESTON COLONIAL

Like the New England Colonial, the Front Gable, Charleston Colonial or English Colonial evolved from the Cape Cod style and were first built in the 1700's.

This 2-1/2 story box-like house has a protruding front wing, which distinguishes the style from a New England Colonial. The wing is often made of cut stone with stone columns on four corners. Exterior features include gable roofs, a cornice on the front or on all four sides, and double-hung windows featuring small panes of glass. A fan light and a side light graces the central entrance in the front wing.

Cold Boiled Lobster Salad
Serves 12

INGREDIENTS

3	lbs. lobster meat, cooked
1 1/2	c. chopped celery
1	c. mayonnaise
	lemon juice
	white pepper
	lettuce
5	tomatoes, quartered
5	lemons, cut in wedges
	ripe olives
	avocado slices

DIRECTIONS

Cut lobster meat into small pieces.
Mix gently with celery and enough mayonnaise to moisten.
Season with lemon juice and white pepper.
Arrange lettuce on a large serving platter and heap with lobster.
Surround with quartered tomatoes and lemon wedges.
Cover and chill for 30 minutes.
Top with 6 tablespoons of dressing (see below).
Serve the remaining dressing on the side as a condiment.
Garnish salad with ripe olives and avocado slices.

Dressing
(Makes 3 cups)

2	c. mayonnaise
2/3	c. chili sauce
2	T. grated onion
2	T. minced parsley
1 1/2	t. Worcestershire sauce
4	T. lemon juice
	white pepper

Mix all the ingredients together.
Cover and chill.

Preparation time: 1/2 hr.
Total time: 1 hour
Skill level: Elementary

LOG CABIN

The first extensive use of the log cabin in America was by Swedish immigrants, and early pioneers. There are two basic types of log cabins. One is built with round logs like the Lincoln cabin and the other is built with squared-off logs like the cabin pictured here. In both cases, the logs are unfinished.

Rectangular in shape, the Log Cabin is usually one story with a shingle-covered gable roof and chimneys at both ends. There are few windows with small panes of glass. More elaborate log cabins are often found in vacation areas where a rustic look is combined with the informal and convenient open floor plan.

Caraway Cheese Log
Serves 12

INGREDIENTS

1	8 oz. pkg. cream cheese, softened
1/3	c. whipping cream
3 1/2	c. Monterey Jack cheese, shredded
1	T. caraway seeds
1/4	c. Parmesan cheese

DIRECTIONS

Blend the cream cheese with the whipping cream; beat until fluffy.

Add 3 cups of the Monterey Jack cheese and the caraway seeds; mix.

Sprinkle the Parmesan cheese on a sheet of wax paper.

Spoon the cheese mixture onto the wax paper.

Shape the mixture into a log, coating the outside with the remaining shredded cheese. (If the mixture is too soft to handle, chill a short time until you can shape it.)

Chill the log for 2 hours or more.

Serve with crackers.

Preparation time: 1/2 hour
Total time: 2-1/2 hours
Skill level: Elementary

35

Orange Sherbet
Serves 12

INGREDIENTS

12 oranges
2   lemons
2   c. sugar
    few grains salt
4   c. water
2   egg whites

DIRECTIONS

Extract the juices from the fruit and strain.
Combine the sugar, salt and water.
Heat to boiling and boil for 5 minutes.
Cool to room temperature.
Add the fruit juices.
Freeze partially.
Beat the egg whites until stiff.
Fold in the beaten eggs whites.
Freeze again until firm.

Preparation time: 3 hours
Total time: 8 hours
Skill level: Elementary

Lemonade Ice Tea
Makes 16 - 8 oz. servings

2 12 oz. frozen
lemonade
concentrate
ice tea mix
(to make 4 quarts)
mint sprigs

DIRECTIONS

Prepare the lemonade according to package directions.
Mix in the undiluted ice tea mix.
Serve with sprigs of mint.

Notes

DINNER AT EIGHT

The cool damp English climate encouraged a tradition of hearty dinners, based on favorite combinations of meat and potatoes.

These recipes reflect English culinary history particularly the bread, called Sally Lunn. Sally sold her warm crumbly bread in the streets of Bath by "crying" her name. Later, a baker and musician bought her business and wrote a popular song about her. Sally has a place in the Oxford English Dictionary and her name was a household word in Colonial America.

COTSWOLD COTTAGE

The Cotswold Cottage was first built in the Cotswold Hills of England at the time of the Norman conquest in 1066. The romantic "cotwold" or "cottage in a wood" became very popular in the U.S. during the 1920's and 1930's.

The smallest of the English styles, the Cotswold is also called an Ann Hathaway or Hansel and Gretel Cottage. It is a ground-hugging, asymmetrical style with a prominent brick or stone chimney.

Other interesting features of the Cotswold are a steep gable roof with complex lines, casement windows, dormer windows and rooms that tend to be small and irregularly shaped.

Cottage Fried Potatoes
Serves 8

INGREDIENTS

5	T. butter or margarine
4	T. shortening
12	medium potatoes (cooked, pared and sliced thin)
2	t. salt
1/4	t. pepper

DIRECTIONS

Melt butter and shortening in a large skillet over low heat.

Arrange the potato slices in the hot shortening.

Season with salt and pepper.

Cook over low heat until the bottom is brown and crusty.

Turn the potatoes and cook until brown.

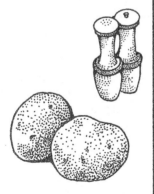

Preparation time: 1 hour
Total time: 1 hour
Skill level: Elementary

ELIZABETHAN OR HALF TIMBER

These spacious houses were erected in England throughout the prosperous reign of Queen Elizabeth (1558-1603), particularly in the London area. The protruding second story, supported by wooden brackets, was a response to narrow London lots where extra space could be obtained by overhanging the street.

The Elizabethan or Half Timber is 2 or 2-1/2 stories, made of stone and stucco, with half timbers. The massive sculptured chimneys, complicated high peaked roofs and small leaded-glass casement windows give these houses their own unique style. The interior often features large halls and a handsome living room with a large fireplace and beamed ceilings.

Roast Beef Au Jus
Serves 8

INGREDIENTS

4-5 lbs. rib roast
    salt and pepper

DIRECTIONS

Place the meat fat side up in a roasting pan. With a rib roast, the ribs will form a natural rack.

Season with salt and pepper.

Insert the meat thermometer so that the tip is in the center of the thickest part of the meat and does not touch bone or fat.

Do not add water, cover, or baste.

Roast the meat in a 325 degree oven.

Thermometer

Degrees	Cooking Hours
140 - rare	2-1/4 to 2-1/2
160 - medium	2-3/4 to 3
170 - well done	3-1/4 to 3-1/2

Remove the roast from the oven when your thermometer registers 5 to 10 degrees **lower** than desired doneness. The roast will continue to cook for a few minutes after removal from the oven.

Allow 15 to 20 minutes for the roast to "set" for easier carving.

Skim the fat from the pan drippings and serve hot, natural meat juices with the roast. (Do not thicken.)

Preparation time: 15 min.
Total time: 2-1/2 to 4 hours
Skill level: Elementary

43

Roast Beef Au Jus
Serves 8

INGREDIENTS

4-5 lbs. rib roast
    salt and pepper

DIRECTIONS

Place the meat fat side up in a roasting pan. With a rib roast, the ribs will form a natural rack.

Season with salt and pepper.

Insert the meat thermometer so that the tip is in the center of the thickest part of the meat and does not touch bone or fat.

Do not add water, cover, or baste.

Roast the meat in a 325 degree oven.

Thermometer

Degrees	Cooking Hours
140 - rare	2-1/4 to 2-1/2
160 - medium	2-3/4 to 3
170 - well done	3-1/4 to 3-1/2

Remove the roast from the oven when your thermometer registers 5 to 10 degrees **lower** than desired doneness. The roast will continue to cook for a few minutes after removal from the oven.

Allow 15 to 20 minutes for the roast to "set" for easier carving.

Skim the fat from the pan drippings and serve hot, natural meat juices with the roast. (Do not thicken.)

Preparation time: 15 min.
Total time: 2-1/2 to 4 hours
Skill level: Elementary

43

Cream of Oyster and Spinach Soup
Serves 8

INGREDIENTS

3/4	quart oysters
1	lb. fresh spinach
3	T. butter
1/2	c. chopped onions
1	celery stalk, finely chopped
3	T. flour
1/4	t. garlic salt
	pinch nutmeg
1	t. steak sauce
	salt and pepper
1	pint milk
1	pint light cream

DIRECTIONS

Cook the oysters in 1-1/2 cups of water until they are firm; drain and reserve the liquid, keeping it hot.

Purée the oysters in a blender or pass them through a sieve.

Cook the spinach until it is well done, then drain well.

Purée the spinach in a blender or pass through a sieve.

Melt the butter over medium heat; add the onions and celery, stirring constantly.

Move the onions and celery to one side of the pan; sprinkle flour over the butter and stir to make a paste.

Pour in the hot oyster liquid and stir until consistency is smooth.

Cook uncovered for 30 minutes and then strain.

Return to heat and simmer.

Add the puréed oysters and spinach to the simmering liquid.

Add garlic salt, nutmeg, steak sauce, and salt and pepper to taste.

Add the milk and cream and cook over low heat for 5 to 10 minutes, but do not boil.

Serve immediately.

Preparation time: 1 hour
Total time: 2 hours
Skill level: Elementary

WILLIAMSBURG GEORGIAN OR EARLY GEORGIAN

Williamsburg, Virginia was the cultural and political capital of the Colonies during much of the 1700's. Houses there were based on styles developed in England during the reign of the four King Georges. Early Georgian houses had simple exterior lines and fewer decorative devices than late Georgian homes.

Most were 2 or 3-story rectangular houses with two large chimneys rising high above the roof at each end. Sliding double-hung windows with small panes and a simple front entrance accented the structure.

Sally Lunn
Serves 8

INGREDIENTS

1	c. milk
1/2	c. shortening
4	c. sifted all-purpose flour
1/3	c. sugar
2 1/4	t. salt
2	pkgs. active dry yeast
3	eggs

DIRECTIONS

Heat the milk, shortening and 1/4 cup water until very warm, about 120 degrees. The shortening does not need to melt.

Blend 1-1/3 cups flour, sugar, salt and dry yeast in a large mixing bowl.

Blend the warm liquid mixture into the flour mixture.

Beat for 2 minutes at medium speed with an electric mixer, scraping the sides of the bowl occasionally.

Add 2/3 cup flour and the eggs, gradually; beat 2 minutes on high.

Add the remaining flour and mix well, until batter is thick but not stiff.

Cover and let rise in a warm, draft-free place at about 85 degrees until double in bulk, about 1-1/4 hours.

Punch down with a spatula.

Grease a 10-inch tube cake pan or bundt pan.

Turn the mixture into the pan, and let it rise again until it has increased 50% in bulk — about 30 minutes.

Preheat the oven to 350 degrees for 10 minutes.

Bake at 350 degrees for 40-50 minutes, or until brown.

Cool 20 minutes before serving.

Preparation time: 1 hour
Total time: 3 hours
Skill level: Intermediate

REGENCY

The Regency style reached its peak of popularity in England between 1810 and 1820. Many of these lovely houses were built in the U.S. in the late 1800's, during the 1900's and they are still being built today.

This style features a spacious 2 or 3-story symmetrical house with a hip roof. A small octagonal window over the front door is very traditional. Almost always of brick, and often painted white, the Regency style has a chimney on one side, double-hung windows, and shutters which are the same size as the windows, giving the house a simple and informal look.

48

Regency Salad Dressing
Serves 8-12

INGREDIENTS

1 T. all-purpose flour
2 c. chicken stock
1 T. onion, finely chopped
1/2 clove garlic
1/2 c. olive oil
1/2 c. vinegar
2 T. French prepared mustard
salt and pepper
1 egg yolk, beaten

DIRECTIONS

Mix the flour thoroughly with 1/2 cup of chicken stock.

Bring the remaining chicken stock to a boil.

Stir in the flour mixture.

Cook 5 minutes over medium heat, stirring constantly; remove from heat.

Purée the onion and garlic in 1/4 cup of olive oil in a blender; transfer to a mixing bowl.

Add the vinegar, mustard, seasonings and egg yolk; mix.

Add the remaining oil very slowly and beat.

Add the hot chicken stock and continue beating.

Cool to room temperature.

Refrigerate for at least 1/2 hour before serving.

Preparation time: 1/2 hour
Total time: 1-1/2 hours
Skill level: Elementary

49

GEORGIAN

Popular in England during the reign of the four King Georges, Georgian houses were built in large numbers in the U.S. during the 1700's and 1800's. This house, named Mount Pleasant, was built in 1750 in Philadelphia.

The Georgian is a large, formal 2 or 3-story rectangular house characterized by its classic lines and ornamentation. Brick is the traditional material. Two large chimneys rise high above the roof at each end. A Paladian-style set of three windows decorates the second floor. The front entrance is highly decorative too, with Greek columns and glass lights on the sides and above the door.

English Trifle
Serves 8

INGREDIENTS

8   dessert shells
1   c. dry sherry
1/4   c. brandy
2 1/2   c. fresh or canned fruit*
2   c. heavy cream
1   8 oz. jar raspberry jam
3   c. cooked vanilla pudding

DIRECTIONS

Break the shells into bite-size pieces.
Pour the sherry and brandy over shells and soak 10 minutes.
Prepare the fresh fruit.
Whip the heavy cream with a beater until peaks form when the beater is slowly lifted upright.
Place a layer of dessert shells on the bottom of a large glass bowl.
Alternate layers of all other ingredients as follows: jam, pudding, whipped cream, fruits (about 4 layers of each).
Finish with whipped cream.
Refrigerate 1 hour and serve.

*Suggestions: use pineapple chunks, banana chunks, strawberries, fruit cocktail and other fresh fruits.

Preparation time: 1/2 hour
Total time: 2 hours
Skill level: Elementary

Thanks to Adina Lambert for this delicious recipe.

51

Notes

BRUNCH

Vichyssoise	p. 59
Quiche Lorraine	p. 57
Tomatoes Vinaigrette	p. 55
Creole Chocolate Cake	p. 61
Chickory Coffee	
Iced Tea or White Wine	

Brunch is that elegant meal served between 11:00 a.m. and 1:00 p.m. which is more than breakfast and less than luncheon.

Very often, egg-based dishes like omelets or quiches are featured, accompanied by fresh salad, and finished with a lush dessert. This charming meal lends itself to celebration, and is lovely on a Sunday, for Mother's Day, graduation, a bridal shower, or following a christening or baby-naming.

FRENCH
FARMHOUSE

The French Farmhouse is based on the charming farm houses found in the various provinces of France. The style varies widely, and was most popular in America in the early 1900's.

An informal house, it is 1-1/2 to 2 stories and made of a variety of building materials. Very steep hip or gable roofs are typical. Accenting features of the French Farmhouse include a large chimney, half timbers, and dormers that break through the cornice-line. Another common variation is that the house is built around a courtyard, with two symmetrical wings protruding towards the front.

54

Tomatoes Vinaigrette
Serves 6-8

INGREDIENTS

8-12 thick tomato
      slices or peeled
      small tomatoes
1   c. olive oil
1/3 c. wine vinegar
2 1/4 t. oregano leaves
1   t. salt
1/2 t. pepper
1/2 t. dry mustard
2   garlic cloves,
      (crushed)
      lettuce
3   T. minced onion
      snipped parsley

DIRECTIONS

Arrange the tomatoes in a baking dish (8" x 8" x 2").

Combine the oil, vinegar, oregano, salt, pepper, mustard and garlic in a tightly covered jar and shake.

Pour over tomatoes.

Cover and chill for three hours, spooning dressing over tomatoes twice.

Arrange tomatoes on lettuce before serving.

Sprinkle tomatoes with onion and parsley.

Drizzle some dressing over the top.

Preparation time: 10 min.
Total time: 3 hrs., 10 min.
Skill level: Elementary

FRENCH PROVINCIAL

The French Provincial style originated in France during the reign of Louis XIV (1643-1715) and was popular among the rich who wanted showplace homes.

It is a perfectly balanced, formal 1-1/2 to 2-1/2 story house with a steep hip roof and curved upper windows that break through the cornice-line. The house is usually made of brick with French windows or shutters on the first floor and may include two symmetrical one-story wings.

56

Quiche Lorraine

Serves 6 as a main dish
Serves 8 as an appetizer

INGREDIENTS

Pastry for 9-inch
one crust pie
12 slices bacon (about
1/2 lb.) crisply
fried and crumbled
1 c. shredded Swiss
cheese (about 4 oz.)
1/3 c. minced onion
4 eggs
2 c. whipping cream
3/4 t. salt
1/2 t. sugar
1/8 t. cayenne pepper

DIRECTIONS

Heat the oven to 425 degrees.

Sprinkle the bacon, cheese, and onion in the pastry-lined pie pan.

Beat the eggs slightly, and then beat in the remaining ingredients.

Pour the mixture into the pie pan.

Bake 15 minutes.

Reduce the oven temperature to 300 degrees and bake 30 minutes longer or until a knife inserted one inch from the edge comes out clean.

Let stand 10 minutes before cutting.

Preparation time: 1/2 hour
Total time: 1-1/2 hours
Skill level: Elementary

FRENCH
NORMANDY

This house style originated in the Normandy region of France, where house and barn were one building. The turret was used for storage of grain or fodder, and in medieval times all the rooms were on the 2nd story.

The main characteristic of the French Normandy is the central turret which today usually houses a staircase. It is a 1-1/2 to 2-1/2 story house and the exterior walls are usually brick, stone or stucco. Other features include large chimneys, high complicated roofs and half-timbers for decoration.

Vichyssoise
Serves 8
(1/2 cup each)

INGREDIENTS

1 small onion grated
3 chicken bouillon
  cubes
1 c. water
  salt to taste
2 c. milk
1 1/4 c. instant mashed
  potatoes (dry)
1 c. light cream
  snipped chives

DIRECTIONS

Combine the onion, bouillon cubes, water and salt in a large saucepan. **Heat** to boiling. **Reduce heat**; cover and simmer 10 minutes. Remove from heat. **Add** 1/2 cup milk. Stir in the instant potatoes and whip with a fork until mixture is fluffy. Gradually stir in the remaining 1-1/2 cups of milk. **Heat** just to boiling. **Cover** and chill thoroughly. **Stir** in cream just before serving, beating vigorously with a fork until blended. **Sprinkle** each serving with snipped chives.

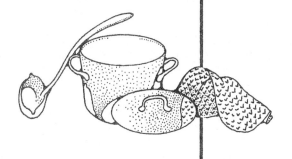

Preparation time: 25 min.
Total time: 8-1/2 hours
Skill level: Elementary

CREOLE, LOUISIANA OR NEW ORLEANS

This house style originated in New Orleans in the late 1700's and 1800's. It appears to have been influenced by French, Spanish and West Indian styles, although it is not found in those places.

A key characteristic of this house is the extensive lacy ironwork running across the entire front of the second story balcony. It is 2 to 3 stories, symmetrical in shape and is often painted in pastel colors like peach, mint and lemon. Baskets of brightly colored flowers are traditionally displayed on the balcony. These charming houses are found throughout New Orleans, but are especially common in the famous "French Quarter."

Creole Chocolate Chiffon Cake

Serves 8-10

INGREDIENTS

2   eggs, separated
1 1/2 c. sugar
1 3/4 c. cake flour
1 1/4 t. salt
3/4   t. baking soda
1/3   c. salad oil
1   T. instant coffee
     dissolved in 1
     cup boiling
     water and
     cooled
2   oz. melted
     unsweetened
     chocolate (cooled)

DIRECTIONS

Heat oven to 350 degrees.
Grease and flour two round 8-inch pans.
Beat the egg whites in a small mixing bowl until foamy.
Beat in 1/2 cup of the sugar, 1 spoon at a time. Continue beating until the mixture is very stiff and glossy. Set the meringue aside.
Measure the remaining sugar, flour, salt and baking soda into a large bowl.
Add the oil and half of the coffee mixture. Beat one minute on high speed, scraping the bowl.
Add the remaining coffee mixture, the egg yolks and the chocolate. Beat 1 minute; scrape the bowl occasionally.
Fold in the meringue. Pour the batter into the two 8-inch pans.
Bake 30-35 minutes or until a toothpick comes out clean.
Cool on wire racks and then frost.

Vanilla Butter Frosting

1/3   c. soft butter or
      margarine
3   c. confectioners'
      sugar
1 1/2 t. vanilla
2   T. milk

DIRECTIONS

Blend the butter and the sugar.
Stir in the vanilla and milk.
Beat until the frosting is smooth and easy to spread. Spread on cooled cakes. This recipe frosts two 8-inch layers.

Preparation time: 35 min.
Total time: 70 min.
Skill level: Elementary

Notes

APRÉS SKI

Cheese Fondue   p. 65
Chocolate Fondue   p. 66
Bread and Cake Squares
Fruit Assortment
Hot Spiced Tea
Rum Toddies

In the delightful tradition of the hardy, winter-loving Swiss, we offer the combination of melting, dunking and communal eating characterized by FONDUE.

Prepare these delectable dishes in a ceramic or metal fondue pot, with a warming candle set below to keep the mixture bubbly and hot. Enjoy around a roaring fire for a cozy, casual meal.

SWISS CHALET

The Swiss Chalet is a copy of the mountain chalets of Switzerland. In this country, they are usually built in mountain areas as ski lodges. The house pictured was designed and built by the late Paul Manchester, a well-known real estate appraiser.

These are 1-1/2 to 2-1/2 story, gable roofed houses with extensive natural decorative woodwork on the exterior. Open porches, large glass windows, and a curved cornice are typical traits of the Swiss Chalet.

The open floor plan, fireplace and hearth, and traditional sleeping lofts make for a friendly communal lifestyle.

Cheese Fondue

Serves 12

INGREDIENTS

1	lb. Swiss cheese, shredded
3	T. flour
1	garlic clove
1 1/2	c. dry white wine
1	T. lemon juice
	pepper and nutmeg (to taste)

DIRECTIONS

Grate or shred the Swiss cheese.
Sprinkle with flour and mix. Set aside.
Rub the inside of a pot with a cut garlic clove. Discard garlic.
Add wine and heat over medium flame on the stove until the wine is warm but not boiling.
Add the lemon juice.
Add the cheese/flour mixture by the handfuls, stirring constantly with a wooden spoon until the cheese is melted and the cheese-wine mixture looks like a light creamy sauce.
Add the pepper and nutmeg to taste. Bring to a boil.
Remove and place on a lighted burner (candle) on the table. The fondue should continue to bubble gently.
Serve with bread squares and fondue forks.

Preparation time: 1/2 hour
Total time: 1/2 hour
Skill level: Elementary

Chocolate Fondue
Serves 12

INGREDIENTS

18   oz. chocolate bars
       (use very rich
       chocolate)
1   c. light cream
4   T. brandy or rum
1/2   t. cinnamon
       (optional)

DIRECTIONS

Break the chocolate into pieces and place in a saucepan.

Add the light cream; melt on low heat.

Add the brandy and stir until smooth and thoroughly heated. (Do not allow the mixture to boil, or the chocolate will burn.)

Pour into a fondue dish over a candle-warmer so mixture stays very warm but does not burn.

Serve with cake squares and fruit sections: pineapple and apple wedges, banana slices, mandarin orange slices, maraschino cherries, fresh strawberries, marshmallows, angelfood cake and pound cake cut into squares.

Preparation time: 1/2 hour
Total time: 1/2 hour
Skill level: Elementary

```
╔════════════════════════════════════════╗
║          IL  PRANZO                     ║
║            (Dinner)                     ║
║                                         ║
║   Fresh Fruit Cup                       ║
║   Mozzarella Anchovy Toast      p. 71   ║
║   Paella a la Valenciana        p. 69   ║
║   Expresso                              ║
║                                         ║
╚════════════════════════════════════════╝
```

In Italy and Spain, the menus and methods of cooking will vary widely, due to local traditions and the availability of fresh ingredients.

In Bologna, the pasta sauce is thick and contains onions, carrots, finely chopped pork and beef, celery, butter and tomatoes. In Naples, spaghetti and macaroni are dressed with an agreeably light, pungent mixture of herbs and tomatoes. Fresh, smoked or salted seafood is used extensively in both Italian and Spanish cuisines.

SPANISH VILLA

American architecture has been influenced by Spanish styles since the days of the Spanish conquistadores. Widespread throughout the warm parts of the U.S., Spanish styles also appear in the North with surprising frequency, despite the fact that they are basically unsuited to colder climates.

The Spanish Villa is an asymmetrical, 1 to 3-story house with painted stucco exterior walls and a tile roof (usually red). The patio is completely enclosed by exterior walls. Arched windows and doors and wrought iron decorations are distinguishing characteristics that enhance the appearance of this gracious housestyle.

Paella á la Valenciana
Serves 6-8

INGREDIENTS

4 T. olive oil
2 garlic cloves, crushed
2 onions, chopped
3 red peppers, seeded and cut into strips
1 small chicken, cut into small pieces
8 oz. pork, ham or beef, diced
5 tomatoes, peeled and quartered
1 1/2 lb. rice
4-6 c. chicken stock (enough to cover)
1/2 t. saffron
4 oz. frozen peas
4 oz. kidney beans
1 lb. cod or whiting, cut into small pieces
1 crayfish, cut into small pieces
6 oz. raw prawns, shelled and deveined
4 parsley sprigs, chopped
salt and pepper

DIRECTIONS

Heat the oil in a very large frying pan.
Add the garlic, onions, pepper strips, chicken pieces and meat.
Sauté until the meat browns.
Add the tomatoes.
Stir in the rice and cook over low heat for 5 minutes.
Add the stock, saffron, peas, and beans.
Cook for 10 minutes.
Add the fish and prawns.
Cook gently for 10-15 minutes, adding more stock if necessary. The rice should be moist but not soggy.
Sprinkle with parsley.
Set the pan on the table and serve directly from it.

Preparation time: 1-1/2 hrs.
Total time: 1-1/2 hours
Skill level: Intermediate

ITALIAN VILLA

First built in the U.S. in 1837, this style was popularized by architect Andrew Jackson Downing in the mid-1800's. Architects Henry Austin and Richard Upjohn also used the style extensively. The Bristol House pictured here was designed by Austin and built in New Haven, Connecticut in 1845.

The Italian Villa is a massive 2 or 3-story house of masonry construction featuring large overhanging eaves and a heavy cornice line with big supporting brackets. Some of these houses have quoins at the corners and many have square or octagonal towers. Decorative ironwork is also common on the exterior of these elegant houses.

Mozzarella Toast with Anchovy Sauce

Yield: 12 slices

INGREDIENTS

1/2	c. vegetable oil
1 1/2	sticks of butter
12	half-inch thick slices French bread
1	T. capers
6	flat anchovy fillets
1/2	c. dry white wine
1	T. chicken broth
1/2	t. pepper
12	slices mozzarella cheese, about 1/4-inch thick

DIRECTIONS

Heat the oil and 1 stick of butter in a skillet.

Brown the bread on all sides.

Drain on paper towels.

Chop the capers and anchovy fillets together.

Heat the other 1/2 stick of butter in a saucepan.

Add the caper and anchovy mixture.

Cook for about 4 minutes, stirring frequently.

Add the remaining ingredients except for the mozzarella cheese.

Cook about 5 minutes over high heat.

Arrange one slice of mozzarella cheese on each slice of toast and place under the broiler until bubbling on top.

Spoon the hot sauce over the melted cheese and serve immediately.

Preparation time: 35 min.
Total time: 35 minutes
Skill level: Elementary

71

Notes

ORIENTAL DINNER

Egg Flower Soup   p. 76
Seafood & Vegetable Tempura   p. 75
Rice with Peapods   p. 77
Pineapple Chunks, Mandarin
   Oranges & Kumquats
Saki, Japanese Tea, Plum Wine

Oriental food has become a mainstay cuisine for nearly all cosmopolitan Americans. Japanese tempura, sushi and sashimi are fixtures in the nouvelle cuisine tradition, as are the light, spicy stir-fried specialties of Szechwan and Canton, China.

Oriental dishes look beautiful and taste complex, but are often not difficult to prepare.

JAPANESE

The Japanese house style was first introduced here in Hawaii and California. It has become increasingly popular over the past 10 years. The classic Japanese house is built of wood, paper, tile, plaster and stone, and is surprisingly similar to functional modern style.

Its construction is modular with exterior wall panels, known as *shoji*, which slide open. Ornamental gardens are often enclosed behind bamboo fences or walls designed especially for viewing from within the house. The roof is made of tile, thatch or wood shingles.

Interior walls also include sliding panels known as *fusuma*. The floors in the living areas are covered with *tatami mats*, which are always the same size, about 3 feet by 6 feet. Family members and visitors remove their street shoes at the entrance of an oriental home to avoid tracking dirt onto these mats.

74

Seafood and Vegetable Tempura

Serves 6

INGREDIENTS

Seafood/Vegetables

18	medium shrimp
2	flounder fillets
10	sea scallops
1	carrot
12	long string beans
1	sweet potato
4	cups peanut oil

Tempura Batter

3	egg yolks
2	cups cold water
2 1/2	cups sifted flour

Seasonings

Grated white radishes
Lemon wedges
Soy sauce

DIRECTIONS

Peel and clean the shrimp, leaving the tail segment intact. Split the peeled shrimp down the backs and rinse under cold running water to remove the intestinal tract. With a sharp knife, make shallow cuts across the underside of each shrimp in three places, equal distances from each other.

Cut the flounder into small sections, about 2 x 3 inches. Cut the scallops into quarters.

Cut the carrot into 1/8th inch thick pieces and the string beans into 3" lengths.

Peel and cut the sweet potato into 1/8 inch thick slices and cut each slice into quarters.

Dry all the seafood and vegetables well between paper towels.

Heat the oil to 375 degrees using a wok, deep-fry kettle or electric skillet.

Prepare the batter by combining the egg yolks and water; mix well. Gradually stir in the flour. Do not overstir; the flour should remain floating on top of the batter.

Dip the fish and vegetables into the batter. Gently drop them one at a time into the hot oil until golden brown (30 seconds to 1 minute).

Remove the deep-fried foods as soon as they are cooked to paper towels to drain.

Serve with soy sauce, a dish of grated white radish and a few lemon wedges.

Preparation time: 1 hour
Total time: 1-1/2 hours
Skill level: Intermediate

Egg Flower Soup
Serves 6

INGREDIENTS

6 c. chicken stock
4 T. Chinese wine or
   dry sherry
2 t. sesame oil
   salt
4 eggs, slightly
   beaten
4 scallions, chopped

DIRECTIONS

Pour the chicken stock into a large saucepan and bring it to a boil.
Add the wine and sesame oil.
Season to taste with salt.
Add the beaten eggs slowly. Keep the soup boiling while adding the eggs.
Garnish with chopped scallions and serve immediately.

Preparation time: 1/2 hour
Total time: 1/2 hour
Skill level: Elementary

Rice with Peapods

Serves 6

INGREDIENTS

1	can (10-3/4 oz.) condensed chicken broth
1	T. soy sauce
1	T. dry sherry
2/3	c. unconverted rice
1/4	c. scallions
1/4	t. ground ginger
1	pkg. frozen peapods

DIRECTIONS

Combine all the ingredients in a saucepan except the peapods.

Bring the broth mixture to a boil, then reduce the heat for 15 minutes.

Cover and cook over low heat.

Add the peapods.

Cook for an additional 10 minutes or until peapods are translucent, stirring occasionally.

Preparation time: 45 min.
Total time: 45 min.
Skill level: Elementary

Notes

BUFFET DINNER FOR TWENTY

Stuffed Mushrooms	p. 81
Pâté Maison	p. 85
Cream of Leek Soup	p. 83
Eight Greens Salad	p. 87
Steak Victoria	p. 89
Baked Lasagna with Henry's	
Homemade Tomato Sauce	p. 91
Gingerbread	p. 95
French Ice Cream	p. 93

Buffet style meals can range from a simple continental breakfast to an elegant full-course dinner, depending upon the occasion.

When selecting a menu be sure to choose foods that provide a contrast in flavor, color, and texture. Crispy foods contrast soft foods, sweet balances sour, highly colored dishes set off neutral ones, a light garnish complements a dark food (and vice versa), and a rich dish goes well with a tangy sauce or relish.

In the menu above, we have included two different appetizers, entrées and desserts to give guests a choice.

EARLY GOTHIC REVIVAL

Gothic architecture was popular throughout Europe from the 12th to the 15th centuries. Many great Gothic churches are still in use today.

Gothic architecture can be identified by the pointed arch of the roof, often repeated in the windows and doors. Early Gothic Revival may only have a few true Gothic characteristics. The house has a church-like appearance and is asymmetrical. Usually only one color and one exterior material are used, wood being the most common, although some Early Gothic houses are built of stucco or brick.

Other distinguishing features of this style are its pinnacles, battlements, and high massive chimneys. Its fragile appearance is enhanced by ornamental tracery.

Stuffed Mushrooms
Serves 20

INGREDIENTS

2 lbs. medium mushrooms
1/2 c. butter or margarine
1/2 c. finely chopped green pepper
1/2 c. finely chopped scallions
4 c. bread crumbs
1 t. salt
1 t. thyme
1/2 t. pepper

DIRECTIONS

Heat the oven to 350 degrees.

Wash, trim and dry the mushrooms. Remove the stems; finely chop enough stems to measure 1 cup.

Melt the butter in a large pan.

Cook the mushroom stems, green pepper and scallions in the butter over medium heat until tender, stirring frequently.

Remove from the heat and stir in the remaining ingredients (except for the mushroom caps).

Grease a shallow baking dish.

Fill the mushroom caps with the stuffing mixture.

Place the mushrooms in the dish and bake for 1/2 hour.

Preparation time: 1 hour
Total time: 1-1/2 hours
Skill level: Elementary

EGYPTIAN REVIVAL

Egyptian architecture was never very popular in America, even in the early 1800's when the fad of copying foreign styles was at its height. The best examples of Egyptian architecture are found in cemetery gates built during the period.

This box-like house features Egyptian columns in front. The windows appear awkward since they are not part of authentic Egyptian architecture. By raising the roof on the columns above the surrounding parts of the building and placing a stone lattice under it, Egyptian architects were able to achieve light without the use of windows.

Cream of Leek Soup
Serves 10

INGREDIENTS

3/4 c. minced leeks
1/2 c. minced onion
2 crushed garlic cloves
4 T. butter or margarine
4 c. chicken broth
2 c. water
3 c. potatoes, pared and sliced
4 c. light cream
salt and pepper
minced chives

DIRECTIONS

Cook the leeks, onions, and garlic in butter in an 8-quart pan for 5 minutes. Do not allow to burn.

Add the broth, water, and potatoes and simmer for 45 minutes.

Purée in a blender or pass through a sieve.

Add the cream and seasonings.

Serve either hot or cold, garnished with minced chives.

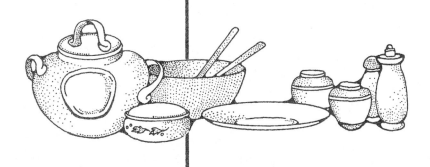

Preparation time: 1-1/2 hrs.
Total time: 1-1/2 hours
Skill level: Elementary

ROMAN TUSCAN MODE

The Roman Tuscan style was brought over from Italy in the 1800's and was used for important public buildings and big city apartment houses.

A house in this style is box-like and fills an entire lot, leaving no yard area. Windows on each floor are treated differently. The roof is flat with a massive cornice. Built of stone, the structure also has chimneys that are small and hidden. Many libraries and university halls are Roman Tuscan style, since the formal, heavy look adds a sense of solemnity.

Pâté Maison
Serves 10

INGREDIENTS

3/4	lb. belly pork
3/4	lb. lean veal
3/4	b. pork liver
1	T. brandy
1/2	c. dry white wine
1/2	t. ground mace
3	t. salt
2	garlic cloves
	peppercorns
4	oz. fat bacon
	chopped red pepper
	chopped cucumber
	buttered toast

DIRECTIONS

Mince and blend the meats.

Add the brandy, wine, spices, and 2 ounces of the bacon.

Mix thoroughly and chill for 2 hours.

Place the meat in a roasting pan containing a 1-inch depth of water.

Place the remaining bacon on top of the pâté in strips.

Bake uncovered in a preheated oven at 350 degrees for 1-1/2 to 2 hours.

Remove the pâté and let it stand, uncovered, for 30 minutes.

Cover the pâté with foil wrap and weigh it down with a heavy object (canned food works well). This step results in a pâté with a close, even texture that will slice well.

Refrigerate overnight.

Slice and garnish with chopped red pepper and cucumber.

Serve with hot toast and butter.

Note: *Never* sample uncooked pork.

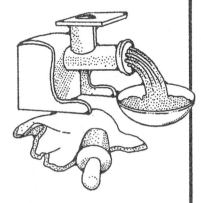

Preparation time: 3-1/2 hrs.
Total time: Overnight
Skill level: Intermediate

OCTAGON HOUSE

Most octagon houses were built around 1850. All were the result of an idea put forth by Orson Squire Fowler, a popular author of the time, who wrote about love, marital happiness, sex and phrenology. In several of his popular books he expounded the theory of a happy life in an octagon-shaped house. He thought that this design made for good interior circulation, heating, lighting, and happy family relationships. Octagon houses were built throughout the U.S. and several hundred are still lived in today.

These houses are built of stone, wood or concrete. Other features include a flat roof with a chimney or windowed belvedere in the center, and a variety of window and door types. A large open veranda wraps around the entire house, adding to its charm and utility.

Eight Greens Salad

Serves 20

INGREDIENTS

Salad Dressing

3 T. salt
1 T. garlic salt
1/4 t. black pepper
6-inch strip anchovy
  paste (from tube)
1 1/2 c. oil
6 large garlic cloves,
  finely crushed
1 c. red wine vinegar
1/3 c. bleu cheese, soft

Salad

6 green peppers,
  sliced
3 avocados, cubed
30 oz. canned artichoke
  hearts
12 scallions, chopped
3 heads Romaine
  lettuce
3 heads Boston
  lettuce
1 T. dill weed
1 c. pistachio nuts,
  shelled

DIRECTIONS

Sprinkle salt, garlic salt and pepper in a wooden salad bowl.
Add the oil and anchovy paste.
Mix well with a rubber spatula until the seasonings are dissolved.
Mix in the crushed garlic.
Add the vinegar.
Mix well until light and foamy.
Add the bleu cheese for cohesion.
Add the green peppers, avocados, artichoke hearts, and scallions.
Tear the Romaine and Boston lettuce into small pieces and place them on top of the dressing mixture.
Sprinkle with dill weed and nuts.
Toss just before serving.

Preparation time: 1 hour
Total time: 1 hour
Skill level: Elementary

87

HIGH VICTORIAN GOTHIC

Most of the High Victorian Gothic houses were built after the Civil War and were based on European Gothic styles popular at the time. The house shown here is the Converse House in Norwich, Connecticut, built in 1870.

Like early Gothic architecture, High Victorian Gothic can be identifed by the pointed arch which is used extensively over the windows and doors. It is much more elaborate than early Gothic, with a great many colors and materials used. The multi-colored effect of the exterior walls is obtained by the use of stone, wood, and brick.

Steak Victoria
Serves 20

INGREDIENTS

1 1/2	sticks butter
5	cloves garlic, bruised
10	lbs. beef tenderloin sliced 1/4" thick
	salt and pepper
2 1/2	t. lemon juice
1/3	c. snipped parsley
	peppercorns
1 1/2	c. chopped onion
1/2	c. cognac

DIRECTIONS

Melt the butter in a skillet.

Add the garlic and brown; then discard the garlic.

Salt and pepper the steaks and place them in the garlic butter.

Cook the steaks uncovered over medium-high heat to medium doneness, about 3 to 4 minutes on each side.

Remove the steaks and keep warm.

Stir in the lemon juice, parsley, pppercorns and onion, cooking the onion until it is transparent but not brown.

Add the cognac and heat for about 2 minutes, but do not boil.

Pour over steaks and serve.

Preparation time: 45 min.
Total time: 45 minutes
Skill level: Elementary

HIGH VICTORIAN ITALIANATE

The High Victorian Italianate style came to this country from Italy, via England where it was very popular in the early 1800's. The house pictured is located in Portland, Oregon, where it was built by Mark Morris in 1882.

The use of three different kinds of window arches is characteristic of this style. These include straight-sided arches, flat-topped arches and rectangular arches.

The house is square with symmetrical bays in front. Small chimneys protrude through the hip roof in irregular locations. Columns support an entablature near the entrance-way and the cornice is supported with oversized ornate brackets, and an elaborate facade.

Baked Lasagna with Henry's Homemade Tomato Sauce

Serves 10 whole portions or 20 half portions

INGREDIENTS

Tomato Sauce

1 1/2	lbs.	ground beef
12	oz.	tomato paste
32	oz.	spaghetti sauce
2	t.	salt
2 1/2	t.	onion powder
2	t.	minced garlic
1/2	lb.	sweet sausage, cut into pieces
28	oz.	whole tomatoes
10	oz.	chopped clams
12	oz.	mushrooms, canned
1	t.	pepper, freshly ground
1/2	t.	minced onion
1/4	c.	red wine

Baked Lasagna

15	oz.	ricotta cheese
1		egg
12	oz.	mozzarella
1	lb. pkg.	lasagna noodles, cooked and drained
1/2	c.	Romano cheese, grated

DIRECTIONS

Sauté the ground beef and sweet sausage with the mushrooms and spices until browned.
Add the remaining ingredients.
Simmer 2-1/2 hours.

Note: This sauce freezes very well.

Preheat the oven to 350 degrees.
Mix ricotta cheese with 1 egg and 3 oz. of mozzarella. Set aside.
Spread a thin layer of tomato sauce on the bottom of a 13"x9"x2" baking dish.
Arrange a layer of noodles in the dish. Spread noodles with 1/3 of the ricotta cheese, then sprinkle with 3 oz. of mozzarella, a layer of sauce and 2 tablespoons of the Romano cheese.
Repeat two more times, ending with a final layer of noodles.
Top the noodles with sauce to cover completely.
Sprinkle with the remaining Romano cheese.
Cook uncovered at 350 degrees for 45 minutes.

Preparation time: 45 min.
Total time: 1-1/2 hours
Skill level: Intermediate

AMERICAN MANSARD OR 2nd EMPIRE

The French Second Empire, from 1852 to 1879, was the period during which this style was popular in the U.S. The mansard roof was originally developed in France in the 1600's by Francois Mansart, as a tax dodge. The upper level was disguised as a roof at a time when taxes were based on the number of levels.

The mansard roof slopes gently back from the wall line and then is topped with a section resembling a hip roof, which is invisible from the street. Multiple dormers protrude through the roof.

Key features include decorative ironwork and mouldings, quoins, and ornate brackets supporting massive cornices. Iron castings are another feature, as are colored glass windows and French doors opening onto porches and gardens.

French Ice Cream
Serves 10-12

INGREDIENTS

12	egg yolks
10	c. medium cream
1 1/2	c. sugar
	vanilla bean

DIRECTIONS

Scald the cream with a piece of vanilla bean.

Beat the egg yolks.

Add the sugar and pour the cream slowly into the mixture, beating constantly.

Cook in a double boiler until it thickens, watching it carefully.

Cool and freeze overnight.

Note: Vanilla beans are available at health food and specialty stores.

Preparation time: 35 min.
Total time: Overnight
Skill level: Elementary

STICK STYLE OR CARPENTER GOTHIC

The highly ornamented Stick stlye is the result of advances in technology during the 1800's. The public was fascinated with the automatic bandsaw, and they used these inexpensive mill-cut parts in great abundance on houses of the period. The name applies to the many gingerbread scrolled houses of the 1800's. The culmination of this fad was the house pictured, the Carson Mansion in Eureka, California.

Exposed framing members, high steep roofs, complex silhouettes, diagonal braces and lots of gingerbread trim give this house its characteristic look. Other features include clapboard siding overlayed with additional boards running horizontally, vertically and diagonally, and complex, ornate doors and windows.

94

Gingerbread
Yields Nine 3" Squares

INGREDIENTS

1/2	c. butter
1/2	c. sugar
1	egg, beaten
2 1/2	c. flour
1 1/2	t. baking soda
1	t. cinnamon
1	t. ginger
1/2	t. salt
2	t. orange rind, grated
1/2	c. light molasses
1/2	c. honey
1	c. hot water

DIRECTIONS

Preheat the oven to 350 degrees.

Grease a 9"x9"x2" pan.

Melt the butter in a heavy pan and let it cool.

Beat the sugar and egg together with the butter until well blended.

Sift together the flour, baking soda, cinnamon, ginger, salt and orange rind.

Combine the molasses, honey, and hot water.

Add the sifted and liquid ingredients alternately to the butter mixture until blended.

Pour into the greased pan.

Bake for 1 hour.

Serve warm or cold

Note: Fresh whipped cream or French vanilla ice cream makes a delicious topping.

Preparation time: 30 min.
Total time: 1-1/2 hours
Skill level: Elementary

Notes

TERRACE SUPPER

Caesar Salad   p. 103
Broiled Lake Trout   p. 99
Welsh Rarebit on Toast   p. 101
Brown Rice with Mushrooms p. 107
Lace Cookies   p. 105
White Wine

A cool summer evening on the terrace or summer house porch is the perfect setting for supper, especially one featuring fresh-caught fish.

This is an informal, relaxed meal for casual entertaining. Enjoy, Enjoy!

EASTLAKE

Charles Lock Eastlake, an English architect, wrote the book *Hints on Household Taste*, first published in Boston in 1872. The designs in this very popular book became the basis for Eastlake-style furniture and houses. The houses, however, were not designed by Eastlake and he was quoted as disliking them in the extreme.

The distinctive Eastlake ornamentation is the major characteristic of this style. Otherwise, these houses look like Queen Anne or Carpenter Gothic. The ornamentation is very three-dimensional, made with a chisel, gouge and lathe rather than a scroll saw. Many of the parts resemble furniture legs and knobs. The Eastlake is rectangular in shape, has a gable roof covered with shingles, a tower or turret, and an open front porch.

Broiled Lake Trout
Serves 6

INGREDIENTS

6	trout, frozen
3	garlic cloves, crushed
1/3	c. olive oil
1/4	t. pepper
	fresh parsley

DIRECTIONS

Preheat the broiler.

Bone the fish.

Flatten the fish or cut into pieces.

Mix the crushed garlic, the olive oil and the pepper in a cup.

Rub the fish on both sides with the oil mixture.

Grease a shallow pan and place the fish in it.

Broil the fish until it is brown, approximately 3 to 5 minutes.

Turn the fish over and brown again.

Garnish with parsley.

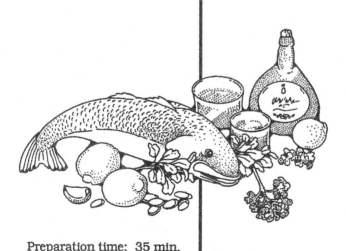

Preparation time: 35 min.
Total time: 45 minutes
Skill level: Elementary

SHINGLE STYLE

The Shingle style developed in New England in the 1880's. It became very popular and many thousands of these homes were built in the Northeast. The style eventually spread through-out the U.S.

The Shingle style house is big and box-like with simple lines. The roof and exterior walls are covered with shingles usually stained or painted a dark color. It has a gable roof, double-hung windows with shutters the same size as the windows, and several chimneys protruding through the roof. Many of these popular homes are still being used today. The Island of Nantucket, off Cape Cod, has mandated use of the Shingle style by zoning code.

Welsh Rarebit on Toast Points
Serves 6

INGREDIENTS

2   c. evaporated milk
2   eggs, beaten
1   t. salt
1   T. dry mustard
    few grains cayenne
4   c. (1 lb.) diced mild
    cheese

DIRECTIONS

Beat the milk, eggs, and spices until blended.

Heat the milk mixture in a double boiler to simmering; stir frequently. Keep covered as much as possible.

Remove from the heat.

Add the diced cheese.

Stir well and cover.

Let stand 5 minutes or until the cheese is melted.

Stir again.

Serve over buttered toast points.

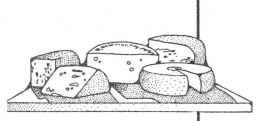

Preparation time: 1/2 hour
Total time: 1/2 hour
Skill level: Elementary

ROMANESQUE

The Romanesque style was very popular in the 1800's for public buildings and churches. It originally developed from Roman principles, prevailing from the 5th to the 12th century. Only a few Romanesque houses were ever built in the U.S.

Architect Henry Hobson Richardson used the style extensively. The house pictured is the Ayer House in Chicago which, unfortunately, was demolished.

This is a massive, stone structure with round, semicircular arched openings. There are one or more towers topped with a dome and it has a pyramidal roof.

Caesar Salad
Serves 6

INGREDIENTS

- 2 c. bread cubes
- 2 garlic cloves, crushed
- 1/4 c. olive or vegetable oil
- 2 Romaine lettuce
- 6 anchovy fillets
- 1/4 c. olive or vegetable oil
- 1/4 t. salt
- 1/4 t. pepper
- 1 T. Worestershire sauce
- 1/4 t. dry mustard
- 1/4 c. lemon juice
- 2 eggs boiled for 2 minutes
- 1/2 c. Parmesan cheese, grated

DIRECTIONS

Sauté the bread cubes in the garlic and the oil until golden brown. Drain on a paper towel.

Rinse lettuce leaves separately and shake or spin dry.

Tear the leaves into fairly big pieces and place them in a salad bowl.

Mash the anchovies with the oil, salt, pepper, Worcestershire sauce, dry mustard and lemon juice.

Pour the mixture over the lettuce.

Remove the eggs from the shells and beat well.

Pour the eggs over the salad and toss.

Sprinkle the Parmesan cheese and the bread cubes on top of the salad.

Mix thoroughly and serve at once.

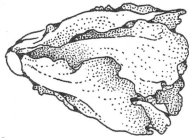

Preparation time: 1/2 hour
Total time: 1/2 hour
Skill level: Elementary

QUEEN ANNE

First designed in England by Richard Norman Shaw, the Queen Anne was introduced here by architect Henry Hobson Richardson in the early 1870's.

The name "Queen Anne" has come to mean any Victorian house that cannot otherwise be classified. These are all unique multi-story houses, irregular in shape with a variety of surface textures, materials and colors. The upper stories of these houses project over the lower ones. There are windows of various styles including bay windows. Half timbering, turrets, and big chimneys are additional features of the Queen Anne.

Lace Cookies
Yields 4 dozen

INGREDIENTS

1	c. all-purpose flour, sifted
1	c. walnuts, finely chopped
1/2	c. light corn syrup
1/2	c. butter
2/3	c. brown sugar, firmly packed
1	t. vanilla (optional)

DIRECTIONS

Preheat the oven to 350 degrees.

Blend the flour and the walnuts together.

Bring the corn syrup, butter and sugar to a boil in a saucepan over medium heat, stirring constantly.

Remove the pan from the heat and gradually stir in the flour and nuts.

Place the pan over hot water to keep from cooling.

Grease a baking sheet lightly.

Drop the batter by level teaspoonfuls about 3" apart. Bake only 6 to 8 cookies at a time.

Bake 6 to 8 minutes until the edges are a light brown.

Remove from the oven and cool for 5 minutes before removing cookies from the baking sheet.

Transfer cookies to a cooling rack.

Preparation time: 1/2 hour
Total time: 1-1/2 hours
Skill level: Intermediate

BROWNSTONE OR EASTERN TOWNHOUSE

Brownstones (also called Brick Row Houses) became popular in the late 1800's in New York and other large Eastern cities.

These houses usually cover an entire city block. They have common side walls with the houses on either side. They are built of brick, often faced or trimmed with chocolate sandstone called brownstone. The roof is flat and the structure has simple double-hung windows. Often, a lower level, called a Boston Basement, can be reached by a half flight of steps down from the street. Eastern Townhouses have a characteristic symmetrical cornice line, although each unit may be decorated differently.

Brown Rice with Mushrooms

Serves 6-8

INGREDIENTS

1/2	c.	diced onion
1/3	c.	diced celery
1/3	c.	diced green pepper
1/4	c.	vegetable oil
1 1/2	c.	sliced mushrooms
1/2	t.	paprika
1	c.	brown rice, cooked
1/4	t.	garlic powder
1	T.	snipped fresh parsley
1/2	c.	shredded Swiss cheese

Basic Brown Rice

1	c.	brown rice
2	T.	sesame oil
4	c.	water
1	t.	sea salt

DIRECTIONS

Preheat the oven to 375 degrees.

Sauté the onion, celery and green pepper in oil in a saucepan until tender.

Add the mushrooms and stir until light brown.

Add the paprika and stir for one minute.

Remove the pan from the heat and add the remaining ingredients except the cheese.

Spread in a baking dish.

Add a few tablespoons of water.

Top with Swiss cheese.

Bake uncovered at 375 degrees for 15 minutes.

Stir the rice in the oil for about 5 minutes on low heat until the rice is popping and light brown.

Add the water slowly.

Stir in the salt and bring to a boil.

Cover the pot and cook about 45 minutes or so until all the water is absorbed.

Serve hot mushroom bake over brown rice.

Preparation time: 1-1/2 hrs.
Total time: 1-1/2 hours
Skill level: Elementary

107

Notes

AFTER-THEATRE SUPPER

The tradition of a light meal after the theatre probably began in the courts of Europe.

While many small bistros specialize in limited after-hours menus, it is often more fun to invite friends back for a personalized repast. The menu must be simple and basic with many items prepared in advance, except for dishes which will, like omelets, be cooked to order.

WESTERN ROW OR TOWNHOUSE

This style is the West's answer to the Eastern Row House. They were built as early as the late 1800's and are still popular today. Thousands of these units have been built in San Francisco and other large Western cities.

Like the Eastern version of the townhouse, these houses are usually built to cover an entire street or block. They have common side walls on either side and the exterior walls may be wood, stucco or brick. The Western Row House or Townhouse is 2 or 3 stories, has a pitched roof, bay windows, and heavily decorated and painted exterior, with a characteristic uneven cornice line caused by varying roof treatments.

Western Omelet
Serves 6

INGREDIENTS

6	eggs
3	T. butter or margarine
1/2	c. minced cooked ham
1/4	c. chopped onions
1/4	c. chopped green pepper

DIRECTIONS

Mix the eggs with a fork until just blended.

Heat the butter in a 10-inch skillet over medium-high heat, tilting the pan in all directions to coat the pan.

Stir the ham, onion and pepper into the eggs and quickly pour eggs all at once into the skillet.

Slide the skillet back and forth over heat, and stir with a fork to spread the eggs over the bottom of the skillet as they thicken.

Let the pan stand over the heat a few seconds to lightly brown the bottom of the omelet. (Do not overcook.)

Tilt the skillet and run a fork under the edge of the omelet; then loosen it from the bottom of the skillet.

Fold half of the omelet over the other half.

Turn the omelet onto a warm plate.

Season with salt and pepper.

Preparation time: 30 min.
Total time: 30 minutes
Skill level: Elementary

111

MONTEREY

Thomas Larkin, a Boston merchant, moved to Monterey, California and built his 1835 version of a New England Colonial out of adobe brick. Most of the other houses in Monterey at that time were 1-story. In addition to the second story, his house also featured a second floor porch, roof shingles and fireplace. The house was widely copied throughout the West and became known as the Monterey style.

The Monterey is asymmetrical in shape with a balcony across the front at the second floor level made of simple ironwork or wood. It is a breezy, easy-living house still popular today.

Zucchini with Monterey Cheese
Serves 6-8

INGREDIENTS

3 medium zucchini
butter or margarine
1 8 oz. pkg. Monterey cheese, shredded
1 c. seasoned breadcrumbs

DIRECTIONS

Preheat the oven to 350 degrees.

Cut the zucchini into thin slices about 1/8" thick.

Grease an 8"x8"x2" baking dish with butter or margarine.

Place one-third of the zucchini slices on the bottom of the baking dish.

Sprinkle one-third of the grated Monterey cheese and the breadcrumbs over the zucchini.

Repeat two more times.

Bake uncovered in a 350 degree oven for 30 minutes.

Remove the dish from the oven and let it stand for 10 minutes.

Cut into squares and serve.

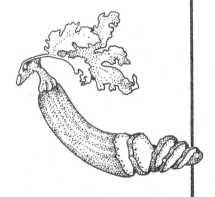

Preparation time: 20 min.
Total time: 1 hour
Skill level: Elementary

WESTERN STICK

The Western Stick house is a regional version of the Shingle style that appeared in the late 1800's. Both Oriental and Swiss influences are apparent in the design. This is a large rectangular house with exposed structural framing and a small chimney that protrudes through the roof at the end of the house.

Other characteristics of this style are its many windows with large fixed panes of glass, sliding glass doors, and a roof that overhangs the house. This makes the house warmer in winter and cooler in summer due to the angle of the sun's rays.

Cold Vegetable Sticks with Dill Dip
Serves 6-8

INGREDIENTS

Vegetables

8	celery stalks
6	large carrots
2	large peppers
1	pkg. small breadsticks

Dill Dip
Yields 1-1/3 cups

6	oz. cream cheese
2	T. finely chopped stuffed green olives
2	t. grated onion
3/4	t. dried dill weed dash of salt
2-4	T. light cream

DIRECTIONS

Clean and cut the vegetables into thin stick-like pieces.

Place them in a container filled with water and store in the refrigerator until ready to serve. This will insure crispness, and prevents the vegetables from drying out. Simply drain the vegetable sticks and arrange them on a plattter with the dip when you are ready to serve.

Soften the cream cheese.

Add the chopped olives, grated onion, dill weed and salt.

Stir in the light cream until the mixture has a dipping consistency.

Chill for 2 hours.

Serve with cold vegetable sticks.

Preparation time: 1 hour
Total time: 2-1/2 hours
Skill level: Elementary

115

MISSION

This style developed in the West in the 1800's. It was popularized as a reaction against the conventional Eastern styles which were being built in the West at the time.

The houses look like the old mission churches and haciendas or manor houses of Southern California. The exterior walls of the Mission house are made of stucco with no sculptural ornamentation and the doors and windows are arch-shaped. There are towers and turrets with pyramid-shaped roofs and parapets which often hide the roof. These houses often have a large patio bordered with a flower garden in the back of the house.

Caramel Flan
Serves 6-8

INGREDIENTS

8	eggs
1 1/2	c. liquid brown sugar
4	c. half-and-half grated rind of one medium orange
1/4	c. cream sherry
1 1/4	T. vanilla whipped cream (optional)

DIRECTIONS

Preheat the oven to 325 degrees.

Beat the eggs in a large bowl with 1/2 cup of the liquid brown sugar until smooth.

Beat the half-and-half in gradually.

Stir in the orange rind, sherry and vanilla.

Grease a 1-1/2 quart mold lightly.

Pour the mixture into the mold.

Place the mold in a pan with 2 inches of warm water at the bottom.

Bake in a 325 degree oven for 1-1/2 hours.

Cool and chill for several hours or overnight.

Boil 1 cup of liquid brown sugar in a small saucepan for 2 minutes.

Remove from the heat and cool.

Loosen the edges of the flan with the tip of a knife and invert onto a platter.

Spoon the cooked and cooled liquid brown sugar over the custard.

Serve topped with whipped cream.

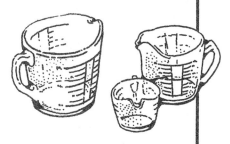

Preparation time: 1/2 hour
Total time: Overnight
Skill level: Elementary

Notes

POST-GAME BUFFET

Spectator sports seem to increase everyone's appetite, especially in winter. This hearty and substantial meal will feed a hungry mob of cheerleaders and sideline heros, in addition to the members of the team.

PRAIRIE HOUSE

Frank Lloyd Wright, who dominated the architectural scene for the first half of the 20th century, designed this style. His total impact is yet to be fully measured. Unlike many contemporary architects, he was vitally interested in home design. The Robie House pictured here was built in Chicago in 1909 and is one of the most famous Frank Lloyd Wright houses.

A long, low roof line, continuous row of windows and an unornamented exterior distinguish this house. Designed to satisfy the physical and psychological needs of the inhabitants, it is unlike the traditional concept of a house subdivided into small boxes (rooms) each with some doors and windows. Rather, the Prairie House is made up of individual areas whose size, lighting and function vary. Many feel it is housing at its best.

Chuckwagon Carrots
Serves 6-8

INGREDIENTS

6   c. carrots sliced 1/4"
3/4   c. butter
1/2   c. bacon, cooked and crumbled (optional)
1/4   c. chopped onion
2   T. firmly packed brown sugar
1/2   t. salt
1/4   t. pepper
  chives

DIRECTIONS

Boil 1-1/2 cups of water in a 4 quart saucepan.

Add the carrots and cover.

Cook over medium heat until they are tender (about 10 minutes).

Drain and set aside.

Melt the butter in the 4 quart saucepan.

Stir in the carrots and the remaining ingredients except the chives.

Cover and cook over medium heat, stirring occasionally, until thoroughly heated (about 5 minutes).

Garnish with chopped chives.

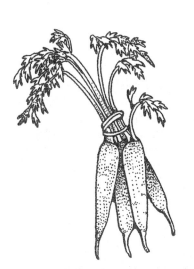

Preparation time: 40 min.
Total time: 40 minutes
Skill level: Elementary

BUNGALOW

Most Bungalows were built in the early 1900's, with the peak of their popularity reached around 1920. The terms Bungalow and California Bungalow were often used synonymously. They are very popular in the shore communities of the East and West coasts.

Bungalows traditionally are used in seashore areas where frontage on the water is very costly. A Bungalow is a small one-story house that usually has an open or enclosed front porch. These houses are narrow (only one room wide) and deep, maximizing living area. They often have an entry at the side. The siding is often wood and the roof is usually shingled. There are many different regional types of Bungalow homes. A Ranch house is merely a Bungalow turned sideways.

Banana Loaf
16 slices (one loaf)

INGREDIENTS

2	eggs
3	T. yogurt or sour cream
1	t. baking soda
1/2	c. butter or margarine
1	c. sugar
2	t. vanilla
1 1/2	c. flour
1	t. salt
1/2	t. ginger
4	T. Grand Marnier or brandy (optional)
2	c. mashed bananas (4-6 medium)
1/2	c. golden raisins
2	peanut butter cup candies, chopped
1/2	c. slivered almonds or walnuts

DIRECTIONS

Preheat the oven to 350 degrees.

Crack the eggs into a small cup and beat with a fork until fluffy.

Mix the yogurt and baking soda in a separate bowl and set aside.

Combine the butter, sugar and vanilla in a large mixing bowl.

Add the flour, eggs, and yogurt mixture.

Fold in the remaining ingredients.

Pour into a greased loaf pan.

Bake at 350 degrees for 1 hour, then reduce the heat to 250 degreesand bake for an additional 35 minutes, or until the bread is firm in the middle.

Cool on a wire rack.

Wrap in aluminum foil or plastic wrap and keep refrigerated to prevent spoilage.

Note: Serve warm or cold. This banana loaf freezes beautifully and toasts very well.

Preparation time: 25 min.
Total time: 2 hours
Skill level: Elementary

PUEBLO or ADOBE

Based on the houses of native Americans in New Mexico and Arizona, the Adobe or Pueblo style became popular throughout the Southwest in the early 1900's.

This house is made of adobe brick or some other material that looks like adobe. The characteristic projecting roof beams are called "viga." Pueblo or Adobe houses are massive looking, with flat roofs and long rainwater gutters called "canales." These homes are well adapted to the hot, dry climate of the Southwest and remain cool and comfortable inside.

Adobe Chicken
Serves 8-10

INGREDIENTS

8	whole chicken breasts, split
8-10	drumsticks
	flour
1	c. olive oil
5	large tomatoes, quartered
1/2	c. slivered almonds
2	green peppers, diced
1/2	c. seedless raisins
14	oz. pineapple chunks drained
1	c. dry white wine
28	oz. chicken broth
1	t. nutmeg
1/2	t. allspice
1	t. salt
1/2	t. black pepper flour tortillas

DIRECTIONS

Dust the chicken pieces with flour.
Heat the oil in a large deep skillet.
Brown the chicken well on all sides.
Remove the chicken and place it in a large unglazed clay baking dish or dutch oven.
Add the quartered tomatoes to the skillet and sauté them for 5 minutes.
Add the remaining ingredients except the flour tortillas.
Bring to a boil, reduce the heat and let simmer for 5 minutes.
Pour the mixture over the chicken, completely submerging the pieces.
Cover the dish; let it stand for 2 hours.
Bake, covered, in a 375 degree oven for 1 hour or until tender.
Allow to cool.
Place in the refrigerator over night. This will enhance the flavor.
Reheat this dish before serving.
Serve with flour tortillas (heat in the oven for 10 minutes.)

Preparation time: 3-1/2 hrs.
Total time: Overnight
Skill level: Elementary

125

INTERNATIONAL

This house style was started in Europe in the 1920's by Walter Gropius, Ludwig Mies van der Rohe and the other architects of the famous "Bauhaus School" of architecture and ornamentation. It was introduced in the U.S. in the 1930's and is the basis of much modern architecture.

The International style is very simple, with no ornamentation. The windows appear to be continuous rather than holes in the walls; some of the windows actually turn the corners of the house. The roof is flat, and the wall surfaces are smooth and uniform. A feeling of serenity, austerity and symmetry is exemplified by its clean lines.

Russian Noodle Pudding
Serves 8

INGREDIENTS

8	oz. noodles
16	oz. cottage cheese
6	T. sugar
2	egg yolks
2	t. vanilla
2	c. sour cream
3	T. graham cracker crumbs
1/2	c. butter
2	T. sugar

DIRECTIONS

Preheat the oven to 350 degrees.

Boil the noodles according to package directions. Do not overcook.

Drain the noodles.

Mix the cottage cheese with the sugar, egg yolks, vanilla and 2 tablespoons of the sour cream.

Blend well until there are no lumps.

Mix together with the noodles.

Pour the mixture into a buttered baking dish.

Sprinkle with breadcrumbs and dot with butter.

Bake for 20 minutes.

Remove the dish from the oven.

Sprinkle the top with sugar.

Serve the remainder of the sour cream on the side.

Preparation time: 30 min.
Total time: 50 minutes
Skill level: Elementary

CALIFORNIA BUNGALOW

At the peak of the Bungalow's popularity, from 1900 to 1920, the name Bungalow and California Bungalow were often used synonymously although one writer of the time classified Bungalows into nine different types. The name comes from the Hindu word "bangla," which means "belonging to Bengal."

A one-story, small compact house, the California Bungalow is usually made of wood. Many of the homes have traces of south seas, Spanish and Japanese influences. These homes are traditionally long and narrow for use on lots where frontage is costly, such as the seashore.

Spinach Salad with Sprouts & Almonds
Serves 6-8

INGREDIENTS

1/2　lb. fresh young
　　　　spinach leaves
1/2　head Romaine
　　　　lettuce
3　T. white wine
　　　　vinegar
2　t. Dijon mustard
1　t. salt
　　　ground black
　　　pepper
1　t. sugar
1　T. grated onion
1/2　c. salad oil
2　c. bean sprouts
1/2　c. almonds slices
4　radishes, thinly
　　　sliced

DIRECTIONS

Wash the spinach and lettuce leaves and pat dry with a paper towel.
Chill the greens in a plastic bag.
Combine the next seven ingredients in a small jar and shake until blended.
Break or cut greens into bite size pieces and place in a large salad bowl.
Top with bean sprouts, almonds and radish slices and toss with just enough dressing to coat each leaf well.
Add more salt and pepper if desired.

Preparation time: 1/2 hour
Total time: 1/2 hour
Skill level: Elementary

129

Notes

THE BARBEQUE

Outdoor barbeques have become a very popular form of entertaining for many Americans, especially in the Southwest and West.

Typically informal events, they feature fresh grilled foods and make-ahead salads and side dishes.

CALIFORNIA RANCH

The Ranch house of the West has spread in popularity throughout the U.S. Today the term is commonly used to describe a wide variety of one-story houses.

A California Ranch is a one-story, ground-hugging house with a low pitched roof. The design is characterized by large double-hung, sliding and picture windows. Sliding glass doors lead onto a patio, usually located in the rear of the house. These houses are often set quite close to the road in front, with most of the lot to the rear where outdoor family entertaining occurs.

Catalina Tossed Salad
Serves 8-10

INGREDIENTS

8 c. mixed greens
(Romaine,
spinach leaves,
Boston lettuce)
3 tomatoes,
quartered
1 c. cauliflowerettes
1/2 c. crumbled blue
cheese
3/4 c. crumbled cooked
bacon
1/4 t. salt
1/4 t. pepper
1/2 c. honey dressing

Honey-Mustard Dressing

1 t. salt
1/4 t. pepper
1 t. dry mustard
1/3 c. cider vinegar
2 1/2 T. honey
1 c. salad oil

DIRECTIONS

Wash and drain greens well.
Tear into bite-size pieces; measure 8 cups.
Add the tomato wedges, cauliflowerettes, blue cheese and bacon.
Refrigerate until serving time.
Add seasonings and dressing when ready to serve.
Toss to coat all the greens.

Honey-Mustard Dressing

Mix the salt, pepper and dry mustard in a small bowl.
Stir in the vinegar and honey.
Add the salad oil slowly while beating with an electric mixer.
Shake before serving.

Preparation time: 1/2 hour
Total time: 1/2 hour
Skill level: Elementary

NORTHWESTERN
OR PUGET SOUND

This style was first developed in 1908 by Ellsworth Storey, a young architect who designed a group of these cottages. The style did not really become popular until after World War II.

A low ranch type house, this home has generous overhangs at eaves and gables, large glass windows and exterior walls generally made of redwood. The roof is covered with wood shingles and its shape reflects a South Sea Island influence. These homes are well adapted to the rainy, humid conditions of the Pacific Northwest, as they maximize any sunlight available and deflect rain.

Seafood Kebabs
Serves 8

INGREDIENTS

1/2	c. salad oil
3	T. lemon juice
1	t. minced garlic
1	t. salt
	red pepper to taste
1	t. basil
1	lb. swordfish or halibut, 1" thick
1	lb. large shrimp
16	scallions, whole
16	cherry tomatoes, whole

DIRECTIONS

Combine the oil, lemon juice, garlic and seasonings in a bowl.

Stir vigorously.

Cut the fish into 1-inch cubes; discard any bones or skin.

Peel and devein shrimp, leaving the tails intact.

Add the fish and shrimp to the bowl and stir well.

Marinate for 15 minutes.

Alternate fish cubes and shrimp with scallions and cherry tomatoes on 8 skewers.

Brush with marinade.

Grill about 5 inches from the heating element until the fish is opaque and the shrimp is pink (about 5 minutes), turning and basting once with the marinade.

Preparation time: 45 min.
Total time: 1 hour
Skill level: Elementary

Beef Kebabs
Serves 8

INGREDIENTS

- 2/3 c. dry red wine
- 1/3 c. olive oil
- 2 T. vinegar
  salt and pepper
- 3/4 t. chili powder
- 2 lbs. beef sirloin, cut in 1-inch cubes
- 8 small potatoes, boiled until tender, and halved
- 4 onions, quartered
- 3 green peppers, in 24 pieces

DIRECTIONS

Combine the wine, oil, vinegar and seasonings in a bowl.

Stir vigorously.

Add the meat, stirring to coat sides.

Chill covered in the refrigerator for 2 hours.

Alternate beef cubes with vegetables on 8 skewers.

Broil about 4 inches from heat, turning and brushing with marinade.

Cook until the meat is glazed on the outside and rare within (about 9 minutes). Cook longer for medium rare or medium.

Preparation time: 2-1/4 hrs.
Total time: 2-1/2 hours
Skill level: Elementary

Notes

CONTEMPORARY
OR MODERN

The Contemporary (or Functional Modern) style is today's version of the revolution in housing started by the great American architects Frank Lloyd Wright and Henry Hobson Richardson and the German architects of the Bauhaus in the early 1900's.

The exterior style of a Contemporary house is an integral part of its overall design. Its function is to enclose some living areas with modern materials yet integrate the indoor and outdoor spaces into one unit. Although there is a lack of ornamentation, the extensive use of glass creates an open, unrestricted atmosphere. These houses are particularly suited for areas of scenic beauty.

Corn Pudding Souffle
(Microwave)
Serves 8

INGREDIENTS

1	T. butter or margarine
1 1/2	T. sugar
3	T. flour
1	t. salt
1 1/2	c. milk
4	egg yolks
16	oz. creamed corn
4	egg whites, beaten to soft peaks

DIRECTIONS

Place the butter in a 4-cup glass container.

Microwave on high for 15 seconds or until melted.

Stir in the sugar, flour and salt.

Combine the milk and egg yolks.

Beat until well blended.

Add to the flour mixture gradually, stirring with a wire whisk.

Combine the mixture and the corn in a 12" x 7-1/2" glass dish; blend well.

Fold in the egg whites.

Microwave on high, uncovered, for 7 to 9 minutes.

Rotate the dish twice during microwaving.

Let stand covered with plastic wrap for 3 to 5 minutes before serving.

Preparation time: 1/2 hour
Total time: 1/2 hour
Skill level: Intermediate

139

SOLAR HOUSE

The idea of a house that would utilize the changing position of the sun became popular after World War II. Several books and many articles were written on the subject. Solar Houses were built throughout the country and the principles of their design are still being used today.

This house has large overhanging eaves and a great portion of the exterior walls consists of glass windows and doors. The house is positioned on the site to take advantage of the high summer sun and the low winter sun. Some models have "eyebrow" eaves that can be removed in the winter.

Sunburst Punch

Makes 12 - 8 oz. servings

INGREDIENTS

46 oz. canned pineapple juice
6 oz. frozen limeade concentrate
32 oz. ginger ale
1 1/2 pints orange or lemon sherbet

DIRECTIONS

Pour pineapple juice and undiluted limeade into a punch bowl to blend.

Add ginger ale and scoops of sherbet just before serving.

Garnish with orange slices and strawberries.

Note: A plastic container or a ring mold can be filled with water and frozen to be used as a block of ice for the punch.

Preparation time: 15 min.
Total time: 15 minutes
Skill level: Elementary

"A" FRAME

With the explosive growth in vacation homes since World War II, millions of families now own second homes that are used primarily for recreational purposes. The simple "A" frame style has been popular in the mountains and near lakes and oceans.

In this style, the frame is the shape of one or more "A's," the house has a steep gable roof which is covered with shingles, and the front and rear have large glass windows. The interior is often roughly finished with a semi-enclosed or loft area used for sleeping, a completely open floor plan and a large fireplace.

142

Asparagus Quiche
Serves 8

INGREDIENTS

2 cans asparagus,
  drained and cut
  into 1-inch pieces
12 oz. cottage cheese
2 eggs, slightly
  beaten
4 T. bread crumbs,
5 oz. Monterey Jack
  or mild cheddar
  shredded
  dill weed
  cayenne
  dried onion flakes

DIRECTIONS

Preheat oven to 350 degrees F.
Mix the first five ingredients together.
Season the mixture to taste with dill weed, cayenne and onion flakes.
Pour into a buttered casserole or quiche dish.
Bake uncovered at 325 degrees for 40 minutes.
Reduce the heat to 225 degrees; cook another 20 minutes, until the outer edge is crisp and the center is firm.

Note: This quiche may be refrigerated until cold, then cut into small squares and served with hot mustard as an appetizer. Frozen asparagus (18 oz.), cooked according to package directions, may be substituted for canned.

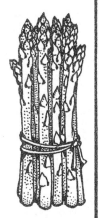

Preparation time: 20 min.
Total time: 1-1/2 hours
Skill level: Elementary

143

MOBILE HOME

During the past 25 years the camping trailer has evolved into today's mobile home. The American housing industry, for a variety of complex reasons, has failed to provide adequate housing for all Americans at a reasonable cost. This gap has been filled in part by the mobile home industry.

The Mobile Home is a relocatable house that averages 12 feet wide and 60 feet long. It is produced in a factory and towed by truck or flat car to the site and installed upon a prepared base. The wheels and axles used to transport the home are removed after installation. Usually the siding and roof are constructed of metal. Often mobile home sites are leased land set in so-called "parks." These homes are substantially less expensive than conventional housing.

Zucchini Boats
Serves 8

INGREDIENTS

4	medium zucchini
4	eggs, beaten
4	T. chopped onion
12	oz. shredded mozzarella
1	jar pimientos, diced
2	c. breadcrumbs
	salt and pepper
	paprika
	butter

DIRECTIONS

Preheat the oven to 400 degrees.
Wash zucchini; do not peel.
Cut off a thin slice at each of the ends.
Boil the zucchini for 10 minutes.
Cool for 15 minutes.
Cut in half lengthwise and scoop out pulp.
Drain zucchini face down on a rack.
Mix the pulp with the eggs, onion, mozzarella, pimientos, bread crumbs, salt and pepper to make a dry filling.
Stuff the squash hulls with this mixture, mounding slightly.
Sprinkle with paprika and dot with butter.
Place in a 400 degree oven until the butter is melted and the squash is heated through.

Preparation time: 30 min.
Total time: 45 minutes
Skill level: Elementary

PLASTIC HOUSE

The Plastic House is not an architectural style in the traditional sense. Rather it is the use of new materials for building. This house is included to represent them all. The house pictured was designed by architect Valerie Batorewicz of New Haven, Connecticut.

A major portion of the exterior siding of this house is fiberglass or other plastic material. Little or no ornamentation is incorporated into this house, which is set into a surrounding landscape with terraces and unusual slopes. The interior features odd spaces, such as a large 2-story kitchen, ship's ladder staircase, and lozenge-shaped rooms which narrow at the ends.

Layered Parfait Mold
Serves 8-9

INGREDIENTS

2	3 oz. pkgs. gelatin, any flavor
3	c. boiling water
1	pkg. (10 oz.) frozen mixed fruit
1 1/2	c. vanilla ice cream, softened

DIRECTIONS

Dissolve one package of gelatin in 1-1/2 cups of the boiling water.

Add the mixed fruit.

Stir until fruits are separated and gelatin is thickened (chill if needed).

Pour into a 6-cup ring mold.

Chill until set, but not firm, approximately 1 hour.

Dissolve the remaining package of gelatin in the remaining 1-1/2 cups of boiling water.

Blend in the softened ice cream. If necessary, chill until the gelatin is slightly thickened.

Spoon over the mold.

Chill until firm - about 4 hours.

Unmold and serve with whipped topping or mayonnaise.

Preparation time: 1/2 hour
Total time: 5-1/2 hours
Skill level: Elementary

Glossary

Bake - To cook food in an oven.

Baste - To brush or spoon a flavoring ingredient over food during the cooking period.

Beat - To mix vigorously with a spoon, fork or rotary beater.

Blend - To combine two or more ingredients thoroughly.

Boil - To cook in liquid until bubbles continue to rise and break on the surface of the liquid.

Bone - To remove bones from meats, fish or poultry.

Broil - To cook by direct heat, (hot coals, gas or electric heat) only a few inches from food surface.

Brown - To cook until the food changes color, usually in a small amount of fat.

Chop - To cut food into small pieces with a knife, blender or food processor.

Cream - To beat until soft and fluffy.

Cube - To cut food into small cubes (about 1/2 inch).

Dot - To scatter bits, as of butter or margarine, over surface of food.

Dice - To cut into small squares (less than 1/2 inch).

Fold - To mix gently with a down, across, up and over motion; usually applied to adding beaten egg whites or whipped cream to a mixture.

Fry - To cook food rapidly over high heat in a small amount of fat.

Julienne - Cut into thin strips.

Marinate - To let food stand in dressing or special seasoned mixture to add flavor or tenderize.

Mince - To chop very finely.

Paella - A main dish of rice, chicken, shellfish, vegetables and seasonings

148

Parboil - To boil or simmer until partially tender.

Pare - To cut off the outer covering of vegetables or fruits with a sharp tool.

Paté - A spread or loaf of ground, seasoned meat, poultry, fish or vegetables.

Punch down - To deflate a yeast dough which has risen by pushing it down with one's fist or a spatula.

Purée - To press through a coarse sieve or blend until food is a consistent texture.

Quiche - A one-crust egg-based main dish.

Roast - To cook meat or poultry uncovered in the oven.

Sauté - To pan-fry in a small amount of fat or liquid.

Scald - To bring a liquid to a temperature just below the boiling point at which bubbles appear around the sides of the surface.

Sift - To put dry ingredients through a fine sieve.

Simmer - To cook food in water just below the boiling point.

Snip - Cut into very small pieces with a scissors.

Sliver - Cut into long thin pieces.

Soufflé - A dish made very light and puffy by the addition of beaten egg whites.

Tempura - Japanese batter-dipped fried food.

Toast points - Toast slices, cut in half diagonally to make triangles.

Toss - To mix foods lightly with a lifting motion, using two forks.

Vichyssoise - A potato cream soup, usually served cold.

Whip - To beat rapidly with a hand or electric mixer, to incorporate air and increase volume.

INDEX OF RECIPES

DRESSINGS: see "Salad Dressings"

EGGS

Asparagus Quiche, 143
Corn Pudding Souffle, 139
Egg Flower Soup, 76
Quiche Lorraine, 57
Western Omelet, 111

FISH AND SHELLFISH

Baked Stuffed Cod Fish, 9
Bay Scallop Bisque, 11
Broiled Lake Trout, 99
Cold Boiled Lobster Salad, 33
Cream of Oyster and Spinach Soup, 45
Paella a la Valenciana, 69
Seafood Kebabs, 136
Seafood Tempura, 75

FRUIT DISHES

Apple Fritters, 7
Banana Loaf, 123
Dutch Apple Pie, 19
English Trifle, 51
Layered Parfait Mold, 147
Orange Sherbet, 36

MEAT AND POULTRY

Adobe Chicken, 125
Beef Kebabs, 135
Corned Beef Brisket, 21
Paella a la Valenciana, 69
Pâté Maison, 85
Roast Beef Au Jus, 43
Steak Victoria, 89

PASTA DISHES

Baked Lasagna
  with Henry's Homemade Tomato Sauce, 91
Russian Noodle Pudding, 127

SALADS

Caesar Salad, 103
Catalina Tossed Salad, 133
Cold Boiled Lobster Salad, 33
Eight Greens Salad, 87
Greek Salad, 29
Spinach Salad with Sprouts and Almonds, 129

SALAD DRESSINGS

Honey-Mustard Dressing, 133
Regency Dressing, 49

SOUPS

Bay Scallop Bisque, 11
Cheese and Vegetable Chowder, 17
Cream of Leek Soup, 83
Cream of Oyster and Spinach Soup, 45
Egg Flower Soup, 76
Vichyssoise, 59

VEGETABLES

Asparagus Quiche, 143
Brown Rice with Mushrooms, 107
Cheese and Vegetable Chowder, 17
Chuckwagon Carrots, 121
Cold Vegetable Sticks with Dill Dip, 115
Cottage Fried Potatoes, 41
Corn Pudding Souffle, 139
Cream of Leek Soup, 83
Cream of Oyster and Spinach Soup, 45
Green Beans and Tomatoes, 5
Hot German Potato Salad, 23
Maple Acorn Squash, 15
Rice with Peapods, 77
Stuffed Mushrooms, 81
Tomatoes with Feta Cheese, 25
Tomatoes Vinaigrette, 55
Vegetable Tempura, 75
Vichyssoise, 59
Zucchini Boats, 145
Zucchini with Monterey Cheese, 113

Index of House Styles

Notes

Notes

Notes

Made in the USA
Monee, IL
15 April 2021